DECONSTRUCTING THE FEMININE

Psychoanalysis, Gender and
Theories of Complexity

Leticia Glocer Fiorini

KARNAC

First published in 2007 by
Karnac Books Ltd.
118 Finchley Road
London NW3 5HT

British Library Cataloguing in Publication Data

A C.I.P for this book is available from the British Library

ISBN-13: 978–1–85575–409–6

Edited, designed, and produced by
Florence Production Ltd, Stoodleigh, Devon
www.florenceproduction.co.uk

Printed and bound in Great Britain by
Biddles Ltd., King's Lynn, Norfolk

www.karnacbooks.com

To Héctor, Daniela and Verónica
To my parents
Presences that are an indissoluble part of my searching

CONTENTS

ACKNOWLEDGEMENTS

Thanks to all my friends and colleagues who encouraged my project, especially to Susana and Arnoldo Liberman, Graciela Abelin Sas and Hugo Mayer, for their friendship, stimulation and participation in the critical reading of parts of this book.

FOREWORD

Letitia Glocer Fiorini is a distinguished member of APA-
Argentine Psychoanalytical Association, where she is also a
Training Analyst and Chair of the APA's Publications
Committee. She is also the current chair of the IPA Publications
Committee. She is an inspired author with several contributions to
the theme of gender. In *Deconstructing the Feminine, Psychoanalysis,
Gender and Theories of Complexity* Leticia Glocer Fiorini offers us a
comprehensive picture of the feminine development in which we can
follow with growing interest several ways of approaching this
challenging issue.

Among it's many valuable insights, this book has the special value
of using contributions from different psychoanalytic authors, as well
as from other areas of knowledge, in such a way that the reader can
follow not only historical contributions, but also recent challenges
as the new reproductive techniques.

In the beginnings of psychoanalysis Freud had the idea that
female sexuality was a "dark continent". From there on, many sort
of psychoanalytic developments had allowed us to have a clearer
and deeper picture of gender structures as well as specific questions
and new situations to be faced.

The theories of complexity shed new light on the understanding
of the feminine. With this book, Leticia Glocer Fiorini offers a
systematization of the current "state of the art" and brings also her
own contributions, as well as possible new lines for future
developments.

I strongly recommend "Deconstructiong the feminine" to all readers interested in psychoanalytic studies, gender studies, human cycle development and to therapists who deal, in their practice with both women and men and their interactions.

Moreover, it is also a very enlightening contribution for a better acquaintance with the high quality of analytic thinking produced in Latin America.

Last, but not least, I am delighted to see that Leticia Glocer Fiorini not only struggles hard to improve and develop psychoanalytic publishing. She is also, and perhaps mainly, a solid analytic thinker and this book offers us many good reasons for rejoicing with the strength of her analytic thinking.

Cláudio Laks Eizirik
November 2007

Introduction

This text is the result of a line of work that I have been developing for several years, based on my psychoanalytic training and practice as well as on my reading and interests relating to women and the feminine in other fields: philosophy, epistemology, anthropology and history. It is part of my interest in the modes of thought underlying conceptualizations of women in psychoanalysis. Advances in the relation between psychoanalysis and the feminine involve considering the complex relations around the question of sexual difference and the always problematic construction of sexual identity.

It is not my intention to offer an exhaustive panorama of the psychoanalytic contributions on this subject or of the main tendencies that other disciplines have developed on women and the feminine. Instead, I attempt to reflect a personal path that I have taken in selecting questions and problems, which is basically related to the dilemmas and questions that come up in clinical practice and the corresponding theoretical developments.

This theoretical review has a guiding thread: the illumination of the *impasses* of binary thought and of the essentialist conceptions of women and the feminine. In this trajectory, my ongoing dialogue with Freud is connected basically with one aspect of his way of thinking: it is multi-centred and complex. This means that I do not take up his works chronologically, nor do I do so for the post-Freudian authors who have worked on this subject.

Each chapter includes other authors with whom I have debated or agreed, or who have enriched my way of thinking. But all of them come into the context of some theme, theoretical problem or clinical matter. No chapter is closed on itself. They all refer, to a greater or lesser extent, to problematic issues, some of which are further developed in other chapters. Certain themes are superimposed, but this was necessary either to accompany a guiding thread through its development or because some concept was analysed in another context, using other reference points.

Throughout this text, questions relating to love, sexual desire, maternity, beauty and the passing of time are addressed. Current debates concerning women, the feminine and sexual difference are highlighted, as well as some controversial topics which have been discussed throughout the history of the psychoanalytic movement. One of the most relevant subjects is the notion of "feminine enigma" and the conception of the feminine as the negative of the masculine. This means going into the nature-nurture debate, as well as into considerations of the feminine seen as the Other of the masculine. I point out that the notion of "feminine enigma" is a displacement of the enigmas inherent in the origins, in the finite time of life (the inevitability of death) and in sexual difference. The basic misunderstanding stemming from this enigmatic condition is the equation of the feminine to otherness.

In the itinerary of the book, there is a progression from the beginning to the end. I begin by focusing on the interplay between different psychoanalytic theories on the feminine and how they impact on subjectivity. Those theories represent different aspects of subjectivity and they coexist in the human psyche. Advancing through the text, the aim is to analyse binary dilemmas, their genealogies and historical conditionings, by means of construction and deconstruction, beyond biological or cultural forms of essentialism.

There is another concept closely related to the category of the feminine: the notion of sexual difference, which is analysed in several chapters. In psychoanalysis, the access to sexual difference is the consequence of oedipal resolution and implies the inclusion of the subject in a symbolic network of social ties. In this sense it is a sort of metaphor which explains the exogamic object-choice for each individual. However, we should emphasize that the notions of both sexual difference and symbolic order are ambiguous and have connotations which depend on codes, stereotypes and ideals embodied in language and culture. The symbolic order is impregnated with empirical and contingent influences. In addition, it does not encompass the broad spectrum of symbolic processes that pertains to each culture and sub-culture. The concept of sexual difference cannot be defined totally in all its facets: it is more of a problematic search than a definitive position of a subject. To this we must add that the notion of sexual difference also implies hierarchical relations.

For all these reasons, these concepts are developed from a point of view that encompasses all of them, in order to sustain ambiguities and contradictions in tension, avoiding false syntheses.

In this context my proposal is to find areas of passage

- through the binary systems to access different types of logics of intersection;
- through deconstruction to find complex constructions;
- through complex configurations to position singular subjectivity.

These are not only theoretical but also experiential movements that occur incessantly. This perspective assumes that we recognize a leftover of ignorance regarding sexual difference, a remnant of indecisiveness that escapes constituted knowledge. It also implies listening to and including the discourse of the Other, so that the Other can become a subject and be legitimated. I believe this to be an ethical response to the questions I am proposing, in the context of an open and multi-centred psychoanalysis.

In the chapter "The feminine position: a heterogeneous construction", my point of departure is the Freud-Jones debate regarding primary or secondary femininity. Psychoanalysis holds diverse and often opposing theoretical positions on the conceptions of women and sexual difference. These include whether the feminine can be symbolized; whether it can have psychic representations or whether it belongs to the category of absence, void, negativity, lack; and connected to these questions, whether or not there is a primary femininity, and if there is, how to conceptualize it. This debate has assumed increasingly sophisticated forms today, with radical conceptions that permeate psychoanalytic theory. My proposal is to focus on the intersection of the paradigm of complexity (Morin, 1986) with the psychoanalytic theories on women and the feminine, in the conviction that the meaning of each theoretical or clinical element changes when the theoretical and epistemological focus varies.

In "The feminine, the pre-discourse and the symbolic", the need to explore domains beyond the "phallic order" is explained. The concepts of gender diversity and primary femininity and their relation to sexual difference are analysed. I include the concept of "additional psychic violence" in relation to the masculine/feminine polarity.

The chapter "At the limits of the feminine: the Other" analyses the relation between femininity and the category of otherness, highlighting the polysemic nature of this concept. I introduce the idea of limit, as conceived by the philosopher Eugenio Trías (1991), as a zone of intersections rather than as a negative element in relation to a centre. The goal is to apply this notion to the intersubjective mother/child space and, on another plane, to rethink the constitution of subjectivity.

In "The feminine in the middle stages of life", I emphasize aspects linked to beauty and forms, relating them to certain crises of life and to the concept of abjection in Kristeva (1980).

In "Love and power: the conditions of love in the Freudian discourse", the point of departure is the Freudian contribution referring to the split between love and sexual desire, which underscores how in the view of ideal representations of the heterosexual couple the feminine position is supported by love while the masculine position is supported by sexual desire.

In "Itineraries of love life", I discuss the paths of love in relation to the categories of repetition and difference. This analysis includes the concept of open systems. I highlight the relevance of the imaginary realm, which overflows the categories of deceit and illusion.

In "Maternity and female sexuality in the light of the new reproductive techniques", I take the contributions of biotechnology in assisted fertilization as a starting point to review conceptions of femininity and maternity. The proposal is to develop a multi-centred mode of thought on maternity that articulates several coexisting registers.

In the chapter "Femininity and desire", I find an endpoint in the conception of sexual desire based on an "original lack". I take Deleuze's conceptions (1980) on desire as production, since it is an alternative path for other theoretical options. I also include another perspective: the concept of imaginary production as it intersects with the field of sexual desire.

In "Towards a deconstruction of femininity as a universal category", the categories of universal and singular are analysed in relation to female subjectivity. The contributions and limits of deconstruction are also discussed, as well as the need to create a *liaison* with operations of symbolic mediation in order to generate new meanings.

In the chapter "Between sex and gender: the paradigm of complexity", the psychoanalytic theories on sexual difference are reviewed, as well as those on gender diversity. I underscore their apertures and *impasses*. I discuss the relations between the trans-subjective, intersubjective and intrapsychic fields, pointing out the need for a complex configuration of the elements at play.

I critically analyse some concepts traditionally linked to feminin-ity, such as those referring to its enigmatic essence, as well as disjunctions inherent in dichotomies and polarities. I develop these themes in the chapter "Otherness, diversity and sexual difference", where I also consider the polysemic nature of the feminine in relation to each of these categories and the lines proposed for the subject's insertion into a context of social relationships.

Work on the knots connecting different types of variables is part of the proposals in this discussion. *The mediations and disjunctions between sexed bodies, gender beings and the subjects of sexual difference are included in these propositions.*

In several chapters I discuss Foucault's conceptions (1979, 1984) on power, which consider the relations of power and domination as constituting human relations. In this line of thought I include the masculine-feminine polarity and point out that it is a source of transmission of identifying enunciations through the bond between the child and her/his primary and oedipal objects, also expressing power relations.

In the course of this text, questions concerning relations between the feminine and the symbolic universe are developed, as well as the concept of lack in connection with a controversial theme: the relation between the subject and the feminine that Modernity has been unable to resolve. The problems and difficulties that came up led me to try to find ways of thinking that would enable me to take them up from different angles. It is not my intention to reach final answers but to point out and reformulate questions regarding certain theoretical crossroads, since I believe that the psychoanalytic theory finds some of its limits and its paradoxes when it faces its relation with women and the feminine.

The binary thought

In my view, the conceptualization of women and its relations with the feminine, in the frame of the theories on sexual difference, remain unresolved in psychoanalysis. There are theoretical problems difficult to resolve: the reflections and questions they provoke are the backbone of these considerations. One of the starting points of this text is the essentialist modes of thought tied to the conceptions of women and the feminine. Some of these are:

1. The binary mode of thought structured by polarities and dichotomies to define the masculine and the feminine. Polarities such as subject/object, active/passive, phallic/castrated, nature/culture, rational/irrational, have been attached in the course of the history of culture to the masculine and the feminine.
2. The exclusive domains that develop these polarities: the feminine linked to Nature, to the emotional field and the enigmatic; the masculine to culture and Reason.
3. The analogies by which femininity is defined in a complementary way *vis-à-vis* masculinity.
4. The overlapping and isomorphism between man/masculine/virile on the one hand and woman/feminine/femininity on the other; also between man, father, paternal function and symbolic function. These equivalences replicate accepted knowledge and discourses.
5. The tendency to universalize those terms that dominate these fields and the impossibility of considering their relative weight in terms of their genealogies and their epistemic roots.

Working on the binary thought implies admitting that dichotomies and polarities are not independent of essentialist conceptions on the feminine. This leads us to consider some current epistemological proposals that enable us to illuminate problematic points. It assumes the inclusion of other modes of thought that focus on psychoanalytic concepts in relation to the feminine position and attempt to include them in broader complexities.

The paradigm of complexity

According to the epistemologist Edgar Morin (1986), the paradigm of complexity is a principle that provides support for new methods of searching for knowledge which can embrace the complexity of the real. It is a form of thought that applies the principle of explanation not only of the order of phenomena (laws, determinisms, regularities) but also of their disorder (the uncertain, the irregular, the indeterminate, the chance, the random). It considers disorder as complex information that will lead to new orders, which are never final. Neither pure chance nor absolute determinism exists. Uncertainty and novelty are part of ongoing knowledge.

Complex thought is neither absolute nor totalizing and always includes a factor of uncertainty. It is not a theory or a technique for application, but a manner of thinking that aims to assume a principle of complex explanation. Complexity opposes totality. It transcends classical determinism, since it considers that there is no lineal relation between causes and effects, and proposes "recursiveness" and circularity to explain phenomena. It creates the conditions for the transformation of vicious circles into reflexive, virtuous circles. This lends support to the concept of process as against linear progress.

Complex thought is multi-centred and plural. In this sense, it exceeds binary thought and radical dualities. It rejects the existence of an explanatory centre, and maintains that certainties are temporary. The paradigm of complexity allows us to go beyond fragmentary knowledge and exclusive disjunctions. It involves constituting relations where there are disjunctions between pieces of knowledge, logical notions and dissociated objects. Those are relations that can sustain not only connections and conjunctions but also heterogeneous categories, paradoxes and contradictions. For this author, it is possible to think in terms of the coexistence of heterogeneities, since they no longer exclude each other if one can access a meta-point of view that allows us to question the initial contradiction.

This is a form of thought that exceeds the limits of Modernity, and enables us to go beyond extreme rationalism without falling into fragmentation or into certain nihilistic variations of some currents of Postmodernity[1]. It is supported by critical judgment as well as open and complex rationality, which is quite different from the indifferent coexistence of ideas that characterizes eclecticism. It focuses on the uncompromising character of certain basic contradictions, and in this sense is positioned beyond dialectics, although it includes it. It permits non-synthesizing connections between two contradictory terms and thus proposes to sustain contradictions rather than overcome them. For Morin (1986), *dialogics substitutes dialectics in an irrevocable way; he elaborates and defines dialogics as an association of complementary and at the same time antagonistic instances.* He lists three principles of complex thought:

1. *Dialogic*: based on the complex association (complementary, concurrent and antagonistic) necessary for constituting an organized phenomenon;
2. *Recursive*: the product is a producer of what it produces in a recursively self-productive circle;
3. *Hologrammatic*: not only is the part in the whole, but in a certain sense the whole is in the part.

He constructs a dialogic tetragram of order/disorder/interactions/organization. We find that this mode of thought allows us to access the Freudian corpus from a multi-centred perspective, recovering its richness and even its contradictory aspects.

The logic of complexity is not the simple, indifferent acceptance of a multiplicity of elements, but the way to make them work together, in collaboration and conflict at the same time. It means sustaining *critical judgment* as a way of maintaining the tensions and contradictions without eliminating any of their terms. We emphasize that this logic is different from the coexistence of thing representations in the unconscious, where opposites are treated as identical, and representations coexist acritically (Freud, 1938). These considerations lead us to make these principles work in relation to psychoanalytic theory and to question the logical, linguistic and cultural conditions of thinking on women, the feminine and the sexual difference.

***

If we return, then, to the question of the binary dichotomies linked to the masculine-feminine polarity, we see that they are seen either as irreconcilable oppositions or as indiscriminate fusions of concepts. In view of this problem, we attempt to find options that help us think about the classical dualities linked to sexual difference from another approach.

1. Taking the concept of limit, the philosopher Eugenio Trías (1991) discusses a new condition in which he considers that the *being* is the *limes*. He describes the *limes* as a tense and conflictive space of mediation and *liaison*. He maintains that the way of thinking about the limit in its negative dimension is worn out and considers it a space with its own legislation. He proposes an ontology of the limit that differs from both modern and postmodern conceptions. The subject is conceived in a space that is neither that of post-modern destitution nor that of the subject of consciousness, self-sufficient and rational; neither confined to the universe of reason nor in the space of the irrational. He postulates a different logical space whose terms pose a problem to the *self-other* duality. It questions the conception of difference based on the centrality of a norm. The extension of the concept of *limes* to the conditions of constructing subjectivity allows us to think of intersubjectivity as an open system in a frontier space of intersections. In addition, considering the limit as a space with its own legislation allows us to depart from disjunctive ideas in which the feminine and women are inexorably tied to nature, the emotions, the affects and the irrational, and the masculine to culture and reason. At the limit, other truths emerge.

2. Deleuze (1980) proposes another path sustained on the concept of *thought in intersections*. His proposal is to generate "lines of flight" to break up strict binary dilemmas. For this author, this means understanding that binary thought may be an essential part of language, but that we also need to produce alternative paths where we can include them and at the same time go beyond them.

3. We also include Morin's proposal (1986) to find a meta-point of view, a meta-system to enable us to find another system of relations that includes concordant but at the same time

heterogeneous categories between contradictory notions and logics. This author maintains that in order to think about the coexistence of two contradictory ideas, we need a "corkscrew" inscription to make the association of antagonistic notions productive. This concept implies generating a solution to replace the classical alternatives.

4. Freudian thought contributes an interesting concept when it considers a non-conventional relation between opposites. Freud reminds us that in Latin, opposites are originally expressed by the same root. For example, *sacer*: both sacred and impious (1938). He develops this concept in relation to the meanings of the uncanny: what is formerly familiar emerges as unfamiliar, as the uncanny (1919).

Thus these contributions generate the project to work with the principles of coexistence, of exclusion-inclusion and of connection-opposition, to deal with the question of women and the feminine in relation to sexual difference and the field of subjectivity. They attempt to recover a dimension of heterogeneity opposed both to irreconcilable dualistic positions and also to the indifferent co-existence of notions. Guattari (1992) points out that the proposal of non-meaning or of deconstruction of meaning sometimes fails to perceive the dimension of heterogeneity of other reference universes. The preceding considerations indicate an itinerary that involves taking a problematic perspective in relation to positive analyses and hasty theoretical closures.

Leticia Glocer Fiorini
e-mail: lglocerf@intramed.net.ar

Note

1. The concept of Postmodernity refers to a fragmentary vision of history correlative to the crisis of the idea of progress, the disappearance of the concept of history as a unitary entity and the end of the great narratives. There are aspects of these positions which sustain eclectic thinking without capacity for linking. However, some statements of Postmodernity contribute a current of relativism which questions the ambition of a unitary, synthetic, closed position inherent in hegemonic discourse. It implies taking into account a multiplying thought directed to increasingly complex realities.

CHAPTER ONE

The feminine position: a heterogeneous construction

The analysis of theoretical and clinical questions related to femininity and sexual difference led me to think in terms of models of thought based on theories of complexity. According to Edgar Morin (1977, 1990), the paradigm of complexity proposes neither unitary theory nor any first truth or master-concept as a key to accessing knowledge. It proposes a circular model of thought which, when dealing with a complex fact, refrains from reducing it to a simplified or mutilated principle. In this sense it sustains the association of two propositions recognized as being true but mutually refusing to make contact with each other; it upholds them as two sides of a complex truth, whose main reality is their relation of inter-dependence. It also involves an organizing principle of knowledge that assigns the same value to articulation and integration as it does to distinction and opposition of the elements under analysis.

Complex thought affirms the coexistence of two heterogeneous notions: order and disorder, as proposed by Balandier (1988). This author states that each order finds, at the limit of its organization, the disordering pressure of the functioning of another order which is foreign and different. In the same way, Castoriadis (1986) develops the concept of *magma* to describe the coexistence of fragments of multiple logical organizations which cannot be reduced to any one logical organization. For Castoriadis, the plurality of the psyche is not a system but a *magma*. He applies the concept of stratification to describe the coexistence of different psychic processes, none of which is either left out or integrated. These conceptualizations, responding to the context of crisis in one-dimensional thought, led me to distinguish heterogeneous orders in the structuring of the feminine position, and to formulate the idea that this configuration is a product of intersection (1994).

The Freud-Jones controversy

Since the origins of psychoanalysis, the feminine has appeared to block any expectation of coherence or integration of the psychoanalytic theory. In this sense, Freud's "dark continent" (1925) expresses the unexplored, the enigmatic, but also, in our opinion, a complexity beyond the phallic register. Its exploration discovers other determinations not homologous to the phallic order. In phallic logic, femininity is interpreted as an enigma.

The debate as to whether there is a representation of the feminine is essential to the conceptualization of sexual difference as a key category for the access to subjectivity. This controversy starts at the beginnings of psychoanalysis with Freud's ideas (1923) on a pre-eminent phallic order ruling access to sexual difference. This refers to a phase where only one genital organ can be represented psychically by both sexes: the masculine, the phallus. Consequently, there would be no primary femininity, and the opposition involved would be phallic *versus* castrated, as expressed by infantile sexual theories. In contrast, Jones (1927) inaugurates another theoretical line based on primary femininity with unconscious representation, which can be symbolized: in this case, the opposition would be masculine *versus* feminine. This debate continues today with aggregated categories, which increase its complexity.

Thus the question as to whether the sexual difference is established between two categories or between one and its lack determines different theoretical lines. These theories oppose and exclude each other mutually, since they involve two logics presented as incompatible. *We will therefore examine the impact of the coexistence of these mutually exclusive and heterogeneous orders on the individual psyche as well as on psychoanalytic theory, since they determine a paradoxical condition in the structuring of the feminine position.* We must add that any consideration of this question needs to include the relation between the subject which is constructing the theory and the theory itself, as well as factors of inertia in collective mythologies that promote a belief in the immutability of structures and theories.

On phallic logic

One of the firmest lines in Freudian thought considers the feminine in terms of negativity, corresponding to the binary opposition: phallic *versus* castrated. Infantile sexual theories are based on this opposition. Children conceive of only one genital: the phallus. Freudian theory contemplates no primary femininity, since it sees the girl's sexuality as primarily masculine (Freud, 1923). These contributions on the one hand present a phallocentric signification, while at the same time generating the potential detachment of the access to sexual difference from any naturalistic determination. There is no obvious access to sexual difference; for Freud it is played out in the differential transit through the Oedipus and castration complexes, whose itineraries differ in girls and boys (1925).

The girl, guided by penis envy, is obliged to change object and erogenous zone, while her desire for a penis, generated by the castration complex, is converted into desire for a child: for Freud, it is the feminine desire *par excellence*. He considers it the aim of feminine desire (1933): if it fails to occur this way, the alternatives would be inhibition or the masculinity complex. Following this line of reasoning, we need to make it clear that the masculinity complex shares overlapping areas with the aim of femininity based on the equation penis = child, since both respond to the same logic. However, since these terms were insufficient, they demanded of Freud a new theoretical element: the pre-oedipal phase, which accentuated the asymmetry between the sexes, though always based on the girl's original masculinity (1932).

At the same time another divergent element appeared in Freud's works which further increased the complexity of the panorama. It is the coexistence of primary masculinity in the girl and the girl's tender relationship with her mother, whom she takes as an archetype; this forms a decisive (pre-oedipal) layer in the oedipal mother-identification (1933). Also, in *Three Essays on the Theory of Sexuality* (1905), Freud already detaches sexual object-choice from what he calls the masculine or feminine sexual character, proposing that full virility is compatible with inversion. Thus he disconnects the circuit of desire from identifications concerning masculinity or femininity, which may take opposite roads.

Lacan follows the Freudian line on phallic organization and sets it apart from the imaginary. The phallus is no longer the penis or even a symbol of the penis (power, potency), but only a signifier without a referent, a place to support desire.[1] He conceptualizes the phallus as a third term (1958a) in oedipal intersubjectivity: the interplay centring on being or not being the phallus, having or not having it, in relation to which both sexes take positions as lacking it through symbolic castration (1958b). We see that in this perspective, sexual difference as such is erased.

However, in his writings Lacan holds to his position on the lack of symbolization of the feminine, accentuating its relation to concepts of emptiness, lack and negativity (1955–56, 1960, 1972–73). Later, he emphasizes the dis-symmetry and non-complementary character between both sexes, and proposes to *mathematize* it (1972–73). The "mathemes of sexuation" are attempts to formalize father, mother, man and woman positions, based on certain modified logical-mathematical formulations. On the masculine side he places the universal, the phallic function and the subject; on the feminine side the denied universal, contingency and the singular: "not all women say yes to castration". In these texts, the feminine position is linked to the *object a*: cause and object of desire. Lacan's formulation "The 'barred' woman does not exist" means that she cannot be placed in a register of universality. In view of these considerations, he concludes that "there is no sexual relation", meaning that there is no complementary adjustment, the feminine position being defined beyond the pale of the phallic register.

Thus, for Lacan, the feminine is positioned beyond the signifying network, exceeding phallic organization. This road leads to feminine *jouissance*, supplementary to phallic *jouissance*, and tending towards the unlimited. This is included in his postulations on the order of the Real, and finally leads to *jouissance par excellence*, as an unreachable and impossible return to the original *jouissance*, to the Thing (*das Ding*): to what is truly real in the mother matheme (1959–60). He considers that women only enter the sexual relation *quod matrem* (as a mother) (1972–73). In my opinion, this accentuates the maternal version of the many paths of femininity. Lacan explains that every subject, man or woman, can be inscribed in any position, be it masculine or feminine. However, I consider that the question of the legislation that so firmly unites the place of subject to the masculine and that of *object a*, cause of desire, to the feminine is left open.

At the other end of the debate, English authors (Jones, 1927) (Klein, 1945) consider the opposition involved as masculine *versus* feminine. These authors argue against the position that the girl is originally a little boy as in the Freudian concept of the phallic phase. In contrast, they consider that there is a primary femininity, penis envy being a defensive formation in response to persecutory anxieties associated with body contents. For Klein, there is primordial knowledge of the vagina, and the desire to incorporate the penis has a receptive-feminine meaning; this leads to fantasies of retaliation by the mother. The concept of femininity becomes positive, but is based on a naturalistic determination: primary knowledge of the vagina. This means that sexual difference would be originally predetermined.

Cultural tendencies, for their part, maintain the masculine-feminine opposition, accentuating determinations provided by society and culture (Horney, 1924). Thus the child acquires a masculine or feminine imprint at birth, without mediation. Phallic organization in the girl would then be secondary and regressive.

Some of these latter currents categorize masculine-feminine polarity, with emphasis on the logic of equality and symmetry; others accentuate the difference itself. More recent gender studies examine the determinant roles of cultural discourse (Stoller, 1968). Other tendencies refer to sexed cues in discourse and search for a specificity of the feminine in relation to language and the body: "speaking in feminine" (Irigaray, 1977).

This summary review reveals several outstanding questions: Does the phallic order encompass the complexity of the feminine position? On the other hand and from the other side, can we maintain that the feminine position is structured only through the initial masculine-feminine opposition, either biological or cultural? How are the ideals referring to masculinity and femininity categorized? Does the process of accessing subjectivity and desire stop at phallic logic as the principal determinant of the sexual difference, or does it involve growing complexities, generating new parameters that we need to register? How do we include the diachronic aspect when analysing the structuring of the feminine position? Discussions of sexual difference mention the enigma of femininity, but is it femininity or the sexual difference that is enigmatic? If it is the latter, then how can we theorize the sexual difference?

In this context, I propose three orders where the question of the feminine position and the sexual difference is at stake: the field of the ideals, the field of desire and a field associated with the wordless, the archaic, referring to primitive experiences in the intersubjective space generated with the primary object. My intention is to show how these orders represent the diverse theoretical developments on sexual difference *within* the psychoanalytic field. This involves discussing their contradictory coexistence, also illuminating the areas of intersection between them. *The hypothesis I intend to develop is that these fields also coexist, in spite of their heterogeneity, in the psyche itself, and that their coexistence determines the subject's "constitution in collision".* These fields reveal the complexity of their structuring. Their modes of articulation involve a passage from one logical system to another. *At the same time, since none of these fields is eternal or a-historical, their determinations need to be de-constructed.*

Femininity in the order of the ideals

The concept of *femininity* turns upon identifying ideals situated in the ideal ego-ego ideal line. We note that this differs from *female sexuality*, which is played out in the field of desire. Also, both femininity and female sexuality differ from anatomical sex (male or female), since their relation to it is neither direct nor obvious. These terms are not always mutually concordant and their divergence is a constitutive condition, both in theory and in experience. We therefore consider that the feminine position should be understood as a complex position structured on the basis of three orders, one of which concerns to the identifying ideals that support the sense of belonging to the masculine or the feminine field.

For Freud (1925), masculine/feminine is an opposition with uncertain contents, which follows and contains others (subject/object, active/passive, phallic/castrated) (1923). He thinks that this opposition, reached in puberty, is determined by different orders: biological, psychoanalytic and sociological (1905), which exceed the purely psychoanalytic. We consider that what Freud considers "uncertain" refers, in another sense, to present theories of complexity. It is important to underscore that Freud includes this opposition in

"The Psychogenesis of a Case of Homosexuality in a Woman" (1920), when he remarks on the disparity between the sexual object-choice and the psychic attitude, masculine or feminine, a distinction already noted in "Three Essays on the Theory of Sexuality" (1905).

From this we can infer that the sense of belonging to a gender, masculine or feminine, implies a "knowledge" about it. But what difference is there between Dora (Freud, 1905), who "knows" she is a woman even though her desire follows a more complex circuit, and Schreber (Freud, 1911), who also believes he "knows" he is a woman? Or between male homosexuals, who have no doubt that they are men, and transsexuals, whose conviction regarding their belonging to the feminine gender is absolute?

If we analyse the orders of determination at work in this dissociation, the first question will be: what is the place of masculine-feminine opposition in theory, and then, can the feminine be symbolized? For this analysis we will discuss the sense of belonging to a gender, basing it on the system of the subject's narcissistic ideals: the ideal ego/ego ideal axis (Dio Bleichmar, 1985). The masculine-feminine opposition operates since the child is identified by its parents, who intervene in the formation of ideals. The narcissistic system of ideals certainly does not derive directly from anatomy or from any kind of mechanical transmission of fixed or immutable emblems by the ideals of culture, which vary with the social imaginary. Nor is there a pre-existing subject that acquires these ideals; instead, they are constituted into an ideal ego based on the parental discourse and ideals which the subject later adopts and regulates as a post-oedipal ego ideal.

On another plane, the constitution of masculine or feminine ideals, as the sense of belonging to a gender, far from being precarious or fragile, is decidedly firm. However, this is no guarantee of this particular identity, just as a subject's heterosexuality is not guaranteed, although the direction of desire is far from precarious. This point brings up several issues that need to be considered:

1.   The complexity of the articulations between the cultural discourse, with its mythical conception of sexual difference, its inscription in the system of parental ideals and the relation to the structuring of the child's ideal ego-ego ideal system.

2. The topic of the symbolic dimension of femininity in this series of articulations.

3. The symbolic implication of the ego ideal as a line that allows us to think of femininity as a system of ideals which are not necessarily a given complement of the masculine but the imaginary expression of sexual difference (emphasizing how the imaginary realm transcends mirroring). The system of ideals corresponding to the ego ideal points to an open, non-immutable system, unlike the ideal ego that sustains the illusion of sameness over time (Mayer, 1989).

4. To the preceding point we add the differing narcissistic value assigned to the masculine and the feminine, based on the castration complex, with all the burden of meaning assigned by cultural discourse. Thus a new order of complexity is introduced into the imaginary constitution of feminine ideals.

At this point we will address some questions in relation to the structuring of the ideals in the ideal ego-ego ideal line.

The ideal ego-ego ideal axis

The constitution of the ideal ego implies assigning a sexual identity to the newborn. It is based on anatomy: the newborn has or does not have a penis, which delineates two fields from a series of notions that are now interpretative; the masculine-feminine opposition is established. Potential ideals are configured which the infant cannot yet internalize.

This assignment is confirmed in the mirror relation with the mother: the child is identified. The mother, for her part, is far from indifferent to her child's gender. Hers is not a simple perceptual recognition of the anatomical difference. On the contrary, the complex process being configured depends on the parents' symbolic-desiring system and its relation to the individual and cultural mythologies concerning the sexes, which are expressed in discourse.

Thus the newborn is assigned a masculine or feminine identity through a name, a certain gaze, distinctive discourse, differential opening up of the erogenous zones (emphasizing Freud's concept of the mother as the initial seducer), all of which will develop different and divergent expectations for girls and boys (Goldstein, 1983;

McDougall, 1987). It constructs a self-image based on the parents' unconscious (Dolto, 1982), which in turn depends on their own oedipal resolutions.

We also need to consider that the ideal ego is structured in a mirrored relation, in an imaginary order where the mother is the place of omnipotence and the absolute, which lends it special potential. Primordial femininity is therefore constituted as an ideal in the narcissistic field and re-duplicated imaginarily in the little girl, because in this case the mirroring is flawless, in the order of the homogeneous. This ideal femininity, which dominates life and death, timeless and eternal, is split off in both sexes when the ego ideal is constituted.

For the boy, it is a particular threat to his masculinity, since it is at the root of the phantasms of masculine castration; it consequently functions as a push in the direction of dis-identification from the mother. For the girl, it threatens her individuality: it implies the danger of remaining enclosed or trapped in the dual relationship with the mother. Thus a field is configured where ideal femininity coexists with the figures of the masculine and feminine genders which are generated through the mother's discourse.

In the order of the ideal ego, femininity is associated with the phenomenon of the double, as a return of the fellow human. This generates the effect of the uncanny: what is most familiar becomes ominous. What is foreign, hostile and taboo threatens to return (Freud, 1919). Fascination with this return, an inseparable part of the effect of the uncanny, is associated with primary narcissism. The ideal becomes persecutory: Freud (1933) described it as the core of paranoia in women.

It is important to remark that the narcissistic identifications indicating feminine or masculine identity in the order of the ideal ego are, paradoxically, *previous to the subject's access to sexual difference, but are also a consequence of this parental recognition*. In this regard, we recall that Freud separates these two orders when he says, in "The Infantile Genital Organization" (1923), that "the small boy undoubtedly perceives the distinction between men and women, but to begin with he has no occasion to connect it with a difference in their genitals". In this perspective, we think that the *masculine-feminine polarity at the level of the ideal ego is not signified in relation to the concept of sexual difference, but as the sense of belonging to the masculine or feminine gender*, on the basis of parental discourse and phantasms. Therefore, this involves a highly narcissistic component.

The concept of primordial, absolute femininity is re-categorized in the logic of the castration complex, in the imaginary figure of the phallic mother. This logic is supported by a conception of desire generated on the basis of an original lack.[2]

In the same way, the narcissistic identifications held for both sexes in the ideal ego, which define masculine or feminine identity, coexist with the primary identification with the father, without mutual exclusion. For Freud (1921), identification has a role in the prehistory of the Oedipus complex; he adds that the boy takes his father as his ideal in a masculine attitude. This, he specifies, is previous to any access to the sexual difference. Further, when Freud proposed in "The Ego and the Id" (1923) that mother and father are indistinguishable before access to the sexual difference, we should understand this proposition in terms of the phallic mother, as a phantasm categorized retroactively by the castration theory, in a Freudian context.

On another front, in terms of the category of ego ideal, we see that the passage from the ideal ego to the ego ideal signals the constitution of symbolic, post-oedipal secondary identifications, with diverse variants concerning object choice which may or may not coincide with these identifications. Access to subjectivity on the level of the ego ideal implies lack, limit, separation and temporality. Far from constituting a homogenization of the model, in the sense of a "frozen" masculine or feminine identity, it singularizes it through a complex identifying assemblage, whose design and combinatory depart from the reproduction of constant schemes.

The imaginary identifications of the ego ideal therefore differ from those of the ideal ego because of the determinations that form a symbolic edge in the former. Subjectivity is constituted as an imaginary system of beliefs, which organizes a sexual identity; this involves highlighting the concept of a foundational image which differs from illusion or simple appearance.

As we have already said, the constitution of a post-oedipal feminine ideal ego re-categorizes femininity; from a narcissistic point of view, it plummets into deficit with the advent of the castration theory. That is, with the constitution of the ego ideal, the feminine ideal falls. This functions as a push towards dis-identification

(Greenson, 1968) and towards the search for a phallic referent, which adds further complexity to the matter.

Thus we define asymmetries in masculine/feminine polarity in the perspective of the ideals, either individual or cultural. These asymmetries are determined both by the mirrored relation with the mother and by the paternal function, as well as by the parental discourse that categorizes what the relation with desire and *jouissance* should be for both genders.

On the other hand, the passage from the ideal ego to the ego ideal concerns the difference between Schreber's "knowing" about his femininity and Dora's. Unlike Dora, Schreber's is the "knowing" of the absolute, omnipotence and the unlimited. It is also the "knowing" of the transsexual who, going beyond most mortals, represents the fantasy of choosing and changing sex. In these cases, the narcissistic aspiration to comprise both sexes or surpass them (the fantasy of the hermaphrodite) carries the weight of the absolute. Disavowal is active.

The structuring of the ego ideal is subject to different vicissitudes relating to the establishment of a symbolic order; its variants influence clinical formations and their variations (hysteria, homosexuality, transsexualism, psychosis). These vicissitudes re-signify the determinations involved in the formation of the ideal ego.

We also need to point out the relevance of differentiating the symbolic secondary identifications organizing masculine or feminine identity as an ego ideal from identification with the phallic signifier, which some authors consider a symbolic operation (David-Ménard, 1987) in this non-sexed aspect, which concerns both sexes and allows identification with the subject's own sex. These two conceptions run counter to each other, and their coexistence bears no resemblance to a unified theory of identification. We see that the plural identifications of the structure configured refer to the same and the different, history and structure, Eros and Thanatos, image and word.

The archaic, wordless: the feminine/maternal

This field concerns registers difficult to represent or beyond the symbolic domain.[3] The ideas of primordial femininity run through the psychoanalytic theory and are categorized by different perspectives.

Different authors describe an archaic, concentric femininity which cannot be represented (Grunberger, 1964; Montrelay, 1974), repressed by symbolic castration. In a different conceptualization, Winnicott (1982) refers to a primary femininity for both sexes which is connected with being and supported by primary identifications. Pommier (1985) attempts to recover certain registers of an archaic, originally repressed femininity when he proposes "being a woman again". Granoff and Perrier (1979) point out the precariousness of oedipal schemes in relation to the variants of feminine histories. Kristeva (1986) postulates a pre-mirror, pre-oedipal register of primary identifications, which she calls the *chora*: a semiotic dimension of subjectivity. This dimension is repressed by the *thetic* or symbolic order, and functions as a disruptive factor. She establishes a correspondence with the feminine, as what is marginal and disruptive in language and the symbolic order. This influences the imaginary bases of subjectivity, since it implies that in every subject there is a splitting of certain archaic and bodily registers connected with the pre-oedipal mother.

Another line to consider in this construction relates to contributions proposing a register of the feminine beyond phallic organization. In these conceptualizations, phallic organization is exceeded or questioned by the feminine as the incarnation of the different, as what perturbs the "norm".

For his part, Lacan proposes a supplementary *jouissance* in women—opposed to any signifying programming—and recognizes femininity beyond the phallic order. He postulates a feminine *jouissance* which is not a complement of phallic *jouissance*.[4] Although this concept can be interpreted in the frame of what is beyond the signifying field but also includes it, the accent is placed on exclusion from discourse, so that this creates a new dark continent: women know nothing about it, nor can they talk about it, as in the case of mystical *jouissance*. For Lacan, this is the register of the Real, impossible to symbolize. Access to this *jouissance*, infinite and unbounded, also refers to "being enjoyed" on the basis of fragmenting, primordial *jouissance*; however, in my opinion this risks making the feminine a myth as the Absolute, thus sustaining an enigma which is impossible to decipher.

All these theories are not entirely comparable since, as we see, some are based on primary identifications while others base themselves on what is not symbolized; still others, more specifically, are grounded in an incestuous *jouissance* beyond the signifying weave. We need to underscore that incestuous *jouissance* should be pierced through by repression so that the subject can access a symbolic universe; however, if we take Winnicott's concept of primary femininity, it should be recoverable as feminine aspects ultimately integrated by the subject. In any case, these categories agree on one point: every subject, man or woman, whether in a masculine or a feminine position, goes through this experience. I consider that calling this field *the feminine-maternal* allows us to embrace a field that includes both sexes. Although this label may lead to misunderstanding, we use it to refer to the initial experiences—pre-oedipal, pre-mirror—with powerful maternal permeation, de-centring masculine-feminine polarity precisely because it involves both sexes.

The primary, bodily, rhythmic, sensory, kinaesthetic, pre-discourse experiences cannot acquire direct psychic representation. This responds to their traumatic character, to an excess of excitations, and they refer to incestuous *jouissance*. These initial experiences pertain to the primary mother-child relationship and are originally repressed, or split off, depending on the author, in both sexes. It is important to point out that although these experiences are at the basis of one of the tripods of femininity, they will be later included in a greater complexity.

On the other hand, I consider that primordial femininity in the field of the ideal ego—as an absolute ideal—is anchored in the reality of this primordial *jouissance*. These are areas of intersection and overlapping between those orders. Like Freud's description of the relationship between the superego and the id, the ideal ego is constituted in an imaginary, mirrored dimension, while its roots penetrate deep into that original *jouissance*. Thus being enjoyed, being identified and being seduced coexist in these initial experiences, though the mother/child asymmetry is never absolute. These are structuring moments that the child will later appropriate as a project. This recognition of the feminine/maternal as beyond the signifying weave, but including it, implies adding another term, which also involves the conditions for constructing subjectivity.

The feminine position as a construction

In all the perspectives I have discussed, it is obvious that the concept of the feminine in psychoanalysis is complex, including contradictions and tensions. In this frame, I used the concept of construction as a metaphor applied to the feminine position (1990). I add that we need to work on de-construction in order to create a mental space of uncertainty that needs to be explored. I refer to the concept of construction in several senses (Freud, 1937):

1. an organization with several inter-related elements
2. a conjecture about a fragment of historical truth, and
3. the working through of what is pre-historic, forgotten and wordless.

This construction refers to the interplay of identifications connected to the ideals (*femininity*) on the one hand, the circuit of desire and object choice (*female sexuality*) on the other hand, and a third order: the archaic, which exceeds the field of desire (*the feminine/maternal*). They constitute heterogeneous spaces, coexisting and sometimes diverging. I underscore that the relations between these fields should be interpreted in the frame of the theories of complexity, which aspire to sustain a productive tension between opposite and heterogeneous forms of thought that are not necessarily synthesizable.

Insertion into a symbolic universe determines the possibility of an exogamic way out through the prohibition of incest for each subject. Also, in a border phenomenon, it determines the structuring of the ego ideal of the same sex. We consider there is a symbolic edge with a dimension of *double entry* in the constitution of the ego ideal: on the one hand parental processing as the initial access to the sexual difference (Laplanche, 1969–70), and on the other hand the oedipal resolution by the child. This implies that the ego ideal is constituted by way of a complex chain of imaginary and symbolic operations.

The establishment of a symbolic order involves a cultural legislation that concerns a third, normative function, separating the child from the mother's desire. This breaks up the narcissistic mother/child universe and thus frames a type of legality based on incompleteness. The notion of symbolic castration, whose versions vary depending on a given culture, refers to these concepts, though it is burdened with a semantic resonance which is difficult to resolve theoretically. In this sense, the equation paternal law = symbolic order requires the dismantling and analysis of the axioms supporting it.[5]

This legality is the same for both sexes. But precisely at this point we need to think about how and from what perspective we categorize the masculine/feminine distinction and the sexual difference—that is, how both sexes are positioned in relation to the three orders already mentioned. We also need to notice the discordance between the feminine imaginary ideals as positive categories *versus* imaginary castration as lack or negativity. For women, this represents a threat to the logic of self-esteem, which should be based on coherent and positive ideals. In the male imaginary, the masculine ideal coincides with the possession of the penis, which is the material carrier of the masculine paradigm. *This means that the constitution of the imaginary ideal is concordant in males and discordant in females.* In this way, the narcissistic structuring of femininity is hindered by the imaginary phallic cathexis that complicates the constitution of a secondary feminine ideal.

The feminine position: a heterogeneous structure

As we see, the feminine position is sustained on three fields that can be mutually divergent. I consider that these fields coexist in the structuring of subjectivity, and that their heterogeneity determines the construction of "subjectivity in collision".

1. A *field of the ideals*, sustained by identifications, in which the feminine primary ideals inherent in the ideal ego (constituted by parental discourse and mirroring) are re-categorized as secondary femininity from a symbolic edge, as the ego ideal. *In this field, the opposition is femininity-masculinity.* We also know that femininity as an ideal is a category not limited to women.

2. A *field of desire*, which signals insufficiency for both sexes when confronted with a third term: the symbolic. In this field, the itineraries of unconscious desire are organized in the frame of a symbolic legislation. In Freudian terms, it refers to the choice of sexual object. When the field of desire is categorized as a phallic order the *opposition will be phallic-castrated.* In this case, it will acquire certain connotations and ambiguities that we need to clarify, since it is neither univocal nor a non-historical concept. On the one hand, it refers to the binary logic

(presence-absence) that is at the basis of the phallic monism of infantile sexual theories. On the other hand, it also refers to the setting in motion of desire, based on the concept of lack that, it should be emphasized, is shared by both sexes.[6] These symbolic operations are categorized by the subject as theories of castration and of sexual difference, mistakenly considering that these analogous concepts are equivalent. This creates a problem resulting from an extrapolation or misunderstanding, by which the category of absence in a logical operation is overlaid with a theory and furnished with meanings. An equivalency is then assumed between the opposition presence *versus* absence, which is a logical and symbolic operation, and phallic *versus* castrated. In this way the categories of woman and the feminine are wrongly equated to a logical category: absence or lack. This in turn leads to a slip that relocates "lack" in the feminine gender by virtue of the highly pregnant imaginary order, which is consequently difficult to resolve.

3. *The archaic, wordless: the feminine/maternal.* We have included conceptualizations referring to what is proposed as not symbolized in femininity. They also refer to incestuous *jouissance,* common to both sexes, but which the masculine phantasms split off and locate in women, when they are categorized as impossible to represent or excluded from the symbolic. *This means that what is excluded from the discourse for both sexes is located in women.*

The following diagram shows the different orders we have mentioned, which reveal distinctive theoretical perspectives on women, the feminine and sexual difference, and which respond to potentially mutually exclusive logics. These different forms of logic coexist in accepted discourse and have an impact on the constitution of the psyche. They intersect with the power of the drive and the field of intersubjectivity.

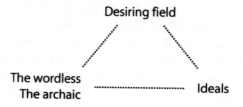

Different conceptions of the sexual difference operate in each of these lines, and each psychoanalytic tendency accentuates one or another. Further, both sexes position themselves asymmetrically in each of these orders, although we are not explicitly considering men's relations with masculinity and femininity; that is, there is no symmetry between the sexes in the order of the ideals, of desire, or of the archaic. This questions the theories that postulate a complementary dovetailing between the sexes.

I would also like to point out that each of these fields is in turn sustained by axioms or assumptions that need to be de-constructed, since they respond to a given conception of sexual difference. *This involves a pendulous task of construction and de-construction.* It further leads us to consider these fields in a broader frame, in order to enable a critical analysis and genealogy of each of them, in an attempt to clarify their suppositions and implications. *In this context we propose to differentiate femininity from female sexuality and from the feminine/ maternal. At the intersection of these fields subjectivity is generated.*

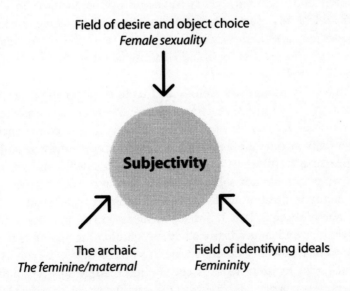

Field of desire and object choice
Female sexuality

Subjectivity

The archaic
The feminine/maternal

Field of identifying ideals
Femininity

The feminine position is organized according to the genealogy of these fields and the ways they intersect. We emphasize that the field of sexuality exceeds the phallic logic of infantile sexuality. We also highlight that *the ways these fields establish relations of conjunction or disjunction with the erogenous body and the symbolic universe indicate the different vicissitudes of feminine subjectivity, which may be more or less conflictive.*

Each of these fields also supports a different discourse on the feminine. In the field of the ideals, the feminine is a positive though depreciated concept; in the field of desire, it is equated to the categories of absence or lack, and in the field of the archaic, it is equated to the unthinkable or the unspeakable, another aspect of the negative.

This creates the need to question the silent axioms of the psychoanalytic theory and to determine the underlying *episteme* concerning sexual difference. As Foucault (1966) puts it, the categories of thought in Modernity are based on an episteme of the Same, of identities, of positive categories and similarities, as opposed to the Other, the different, which must be excluded or ignored. Conceiving the Other as whatever departs from a norm or rule involves two alternatives: either it is included in the norm by diluting its specificity, or it is ignored and excluded, which leaves no option to think in terms of a radical otherness. When we consider an alternative episteme, *we question the assumption that the psychic apparatus registers only one binary, phallic-castrated logic, and postulate that it might be able to deal with the complexity of other logics.*

These contributions therefore lead us to consider the concept of construction as more than a set of elements whose sum organizes a harmonious totality. It can also be conceived as a coexistence of potentially incompatible elements that cannot necessarily be unified, responding to different logics and to heterogeneous orders, with neither principals nor subordinates, referring to the complexity of the feminine position and the risks of defining it or boxing it into any one of those orders. It implies being able to sustain the conflict, its tensions and contradictions without eliminating any of its terms.

If we can consider divergent logics in these fields, we can avoid reducing the feminine to an essence represented by only one of these orders. Also, when we question the establishment of a fixed and immutable relationship between the feminine and the fields of desire, of the ideals and of the archaic, we posit other questions concerning their legislation. In this context, it would also be questionable if the answer to the question about femininity could be reduced, as some contributions have attempted, to women as being mothers, even considering that maternity far transcends the biological domain.

These heterogeneous fields, whose coexistence is paradoxical, contain other oppositions: positivity *versus* negativity, subject *versus* object, universal *versus* particular, complement *versus* supplement and symmetry *versus* asymmetry. In these systems of multiple oppositions, with different but coexisting logics, with variables that oppose but also include each other, the question about the sexual difference acquires even greater complexity. Thus we understand that the paths for accessing subjectivity involve operations of intersection between these fields. Each of them has a different relationship with the symbolic field as well as a differential conception and legislation of femininity and its relation to desire, *jouissance* and the place of the subject, which are presented imaginarily as if they were immutable.

In this frame, we emphasize that access to the sexual difference is a symbolic operation, always problematic, that leads to a psychic construction of the subject's own sex, whose enigmatic dimension is displaced onto the feminine. As a symbolic operation, it is non-sexed, but it is deeply outlined by pre-existing significations. This complexity excludes the possibility of any one-faceted or simplified discussions about this subject.[7]

When we need to think in terms of different overlapping orders and their interconnections, we can turn today to epistemologies centring on the notion of limit. In this direction, I would like to highlight the thinking of Eugenio Trías (1991) regarding a "logic of the limit", in which the intersection of these fields creates a new space of mediation and relation (by conjunction-disjunction). Thus the limit is conceived not as mere negativity but as a space with its own laws, which in turn participate in the laws of the fields that constitute it.

This itinerary shows that the concept of feminine position in the psychoanalytic theory is constructed "in collision". This is a clash between heterogeneous fields, which cannot always be summed or integrated, but coexist in a paradoxical way and sometimes exclude each other mutually. To sustain their heterogeneity leads us to consider all the implications of their impact on the structuring of the psychic apparatus and the construction of subjectivity, as well as their consequences for the practice of psychoanalysis.

Notes

1. The penis-phallus-power equation derives from ancient Asian and Greek cultures and stands today. Therefore, it is difficult to detach the concept of phallus from a reference to its meaning.
2. Cf. Chapter Eight, where we discuss other alternatives which add further complexity to this conception of desire.
3. In this section I am referring to the feminine with a specific meaning connected with the maternal figure, but emphasizing that it is a polysemic notion in which relation to women is not univocal.
4. Lacan's concept of jouissance differs from an empirical sense, and refers to a notion in Beyond the Pleasure Principle. He distinguishes phallic jouissance, specific and limited, from feminine jouissance, infinite and unlimited, which the author compares to mystical jouissance.
5. Cf. Chapter Eight, regarding the given equivalence between the law-of-the-father and the symbolic order.
6. Cf. Chapter Eight. The concept of productive desire (Deleuze) introduces another perspective to this question.
7. Cf. Chapter Eleven for further discussions about the notion of sexual difference and its distinction from the more encompassing category of difference itself.

CHAPTER TWO

The feminine, the pre-discourse and the symbolic

Problems and questions

Continuing from the previous chapter, we will discuss some dilemmas concerning the constitution of femininity and masculinity, their relation to the sense of belonging to one or the other gender, and how this relates to sexuality and the field of desire. We have seen that the Freudian perspective (1924, 1925, 1931) considers access to sexual difference as part of a complex process, incarnated by the Oedipus myth. The relation between the Oedipus and castration complexes is different for boys and girls: as Freud says, boys reach a resolution of the Oedipus complex through the threat of castration; on the other hand, girls go into the Oedipus complex when they find they are "castrated". The concept of castration in Freud is indissolubly associated with the concept of phallic phase: the sexual difference is defined by the opposition of phallic *versus* castrated. To have or not to have; and if she doesn't have it, it's because she has lost it—by way of the threat of castration—is part of the boy's interpretation when he views the female genitals. However, only the conjunction of vision and interpretation produces this effect, and only the existence of a previous theory produces this interpretation. For girls, the situation is different: they discover their "lack" and fall victim to penis envy.

In this process, both need to arrive at a resolution of the Oedipus and castration complexes, in order to make—through the prohibition of incest—an exogamic object choice. In the boy's case, castration anxiety is the motor of his renunciation of his mother, since it

31

involves a threat to his narcissism. In the girl's, penis envy leads her from the mother who deprived her to the father as potential donor. Through the symbolic equation penis = child, she expects to get a child from her father. Disillusionment slowly draws her away from her father, to an exogamic exit that is never as radical as the boy's.

A cut off and a slip: two concepts that guide Freudian theory on access to exogamy and object choice in boys and girls. But who is the individual who falls victim to the threat of castration or to penis envy? The person is a boy or girl who processes the castration complex as a function of their previous sexual identity, as Freud (1923) describes it in "The infantile genital organization" (cf. Chapter One).

The problem is how to conceptualize this difference—which is perceived even "before" the phallic phase—and its entire relation to a diversity of genitals. If the sexual difference is defined in the phallic stage and if, according to the infantile sexual theories, the response to castration differs depending on whether the individual is a boy or a girl, how do we categorize this boy or girl who has fallen victim to the threat of castration or penis envy, depending on his or her "previous sex"? In the same line of thinking, Tort (1991) reminds us that the subjects situated in masculine or feminine positions are previously named as males or females. This means that on the one hand, in the phallic phase only *one* genital, the masculine, the phallus, has a role: "all beings have a penis". On the other hand, there is a boy or girl who goes through the Oedipus and castration complexes in a different way, depending on previous sexual identity.

If the access to sexual difference in a symbolic sense comes into play, according to Freudian theory, in the Oedipus-castration passage, is the boy or girl who is processing the castration complex a biological being, re-defined only *après coup*? What is the place of anatomical sex? What relations are there between biological sex and the erogenous body in boys and girls? What is the role of the mother, a privileged agent in the construction of the initial identifications? In a psychic space which ignores the sexual difference, do these initial identifications also not know whether the baby is a boy or a girl, with his or her diversity? And if there is recognition, is it only anatomical recognition? Further, is the notion of anatomical sex, independent of previous notions of identity or difference, even possible (Laqueur, 1990)?

So how do we conceptualize a boy or a girl "previous" to oedipal access to the anatomical sexual difference, whose identity as a boy or a girl determines either that he is anguished by the possibility of losing his penis or that she accepts a "consummated castration"? How can we reconcile these questions with the Freudian concept of "phallic primacy" in relation to infantile sexual theories which attribute the possession of the penis to both sexes?[1] How can we, unless we accept the false alternative of either re-signification or pre-existing significations? At this point, the concept of re-signification in the Oedipus-castration complex comes into conflict with proposals that support the importance of pre-existing significations concerning sexual difference, mediated by maternal discourse.

Maternal discourse

Maternal discourse, as an expression of unconscious desires, conscious and unconscious ideals and identifying proposals, includes recognition of the newborn's sex. In this sense her recognition involves an interpretation, for which reason anatomical sex is never only anatomical. Different forms of discourse are developed in a relational space which expresses notions about difference and identity as the mother deals with them; the mother's gaze expresses her ideals, projects, desires and recognition for one sex or the other.

Discourses and gazes: on these lines a masculine or feminine sexual identity is shaped; exceptions aside, the newborn is located in one or the other field and identified as a boy or a girl. For Aulagnier (1975), this is a constitutive loss in the construction of the ego: "The field of the identifying references is marked by a disjunction; being a female or a male means that the individual will never know the *jouissance* of the other sex." This sense of belonging to one of two sexes, which is produced by sexual assignation, locates the newborn as a boy or a girl. This is reinforced by mirror identifications, desires, perceptions, a certain maternal gaze, the different ways of marking the body erotically, all of them automatically implying pre-figured incompleteness. This coexists with the aspiration to the One, into which the bisexual phantasm is inserted (Green, 1982).

At this point we find it interesting to include Aulagnier's concept of identifying project (1975). For her, the ego appears as a product of the first identifying enunciations provided by the maternal discourse, which anticipates the child's capacity to understand their meaning. The identifying project is supported by a network of relations which gives identity a symbolic foundation. I would like to emphasize the following issues: firstly the concept of encounter with a meaningful other, which involves relation and movement; and secondly the concept of the mother as a spokesperson, in the sense that she represents an order outside herself, an order whose legislation she conveys through her discourse. Through these anticipatory identifying enunciations, social and external reality are expressed and represented.

I consider that these enunciations cannot omit gender identifications which indicate the sense of belonging to the masculine or feminine gender, and that this process is previous to access to sexual difference. On the basis of this concept, I propose that what we call sexual identity is part of this identifying process-project which is imaginary, but at the same time has efficacy for symbolic projections. So the question is how the ego deciphers the enigmas, desires and unconscious fantasies referring to the sexual difference in parental discourse. The sense of belonging to a gender is supported by mirror identifications sustained by the maternal gaze, and they provide a core of imaginary feminine or masculine identity. The hypothesis is therefore that these enunciations cannot omit masculine or feminine identifications. These identifications, constituted in an imaginary register, mark a *distinction or a diversity of genders*. However, this sector of identifications responds to a *double movement*: on the one hand they are constructed in mirroring, within an imaginary register, and on the other they respond to an external order, to a legislation conveyed by current discourse.

There are two lines that take shape and are not always convergent. On the one hand, diversity refers to the placement on the masculine or feminine side from the identifying perspective. This perspective is never only imaginary, since it is bordered by a symbolic edge, in the frame of intersubjectivity. On the other hand, sexual difference re-defines this distinction through symbolic systems of representation. In this sense, the access to sexual difference represents an operation that allows the subject to be included in a symbolic universe, in the context of a given culture.[2] This symbolic universe precedes the subject, but the subject should insert him- or herself into it, in order to become a subject. Thinking in these terms involves simultaneously examining contrasting elements or concepts which may not enter into dialectics and do not necessarily lead to a synthesis.

We need to make it clear that the concept of *identity* is not sufficient to understand positioning on the masculine or feminine side, particularly if we view this as a fixed, pre-existing identity or, in a logical sense, equal to itself. However, this does not mean that we can avoid considering the imaginary core of gender identity, which organizes the awareness of "being" a male or a female, but which also responds to stereotypes and standing notions regarding the sexual difference as well as to the deformations of mirroring. According to Trías (1983), identity as repetition or pure present is re-defined after the access to difference as sameness. This proposal allows us to think of these concepts in terms of continuities and discontinuities, by including in this frame the categories of repetition and difference.

In this sense, the concept of identifications offers us a field with increased mobility and multiplicity which admits symbolic positioning through secondary identification. These identifications are part of the ego and the narcissistic ideals in the ideal ego-ego ideal line. However, we need to emphasize that the mobility of the ideals is not limitless, since it meets with a limit when it confronts "hard cores" of resistance. The feminine or masculine ideals indicate a "you must be" which creates different psychic spaces concordant with or opposed to the belief in a given sexual identity.

Access to sexual difference in the oedipal sense shapes secondary identifications with a symbolic character. At the same time, this does not happen on a *tabula rasa*, but on individuals who are already girls or boys, not only because of their anatomical conformation but because of the structuring of their mirror ego as girl or boy. *The narcissistic line knows about gender diversity, even though it has not accessed sexual difference.* We should also emphasize that the itinerary of desire always goes beyond gender identity and also exceeds the access to sexual difference.

Gender diversity and primary femininity in the pre-oedipal space

We consider that we need to sustain a double determination: firstly, the determination relating to gender identifications, masculine or feminine, articulated in the maternal discourse with ideals held in relation to the sexual difference. We recall that Freud (1933) says that the relation between the boy and his mother is the freest of ambivalence, and we understand that this already implies a different point of departure for each sex. These observations remain partly in standing, and are more or less marked depending on the conditions of parental oedipal resolution. To this we add that the line of prohibition-facilitation of desire is organized in conditions which differ for boys and girls. In this sense, Josine Muller already said in 1932 that self-esteem depends on satisfactory drive activity. But we know that this is conflictive in women, first because it is not accepted or promoted by parental phantasms in the same way that it is for the boy; second, because drive activity and wish-fulfilment contradict its narcissistic valuation, as Freud pointed out (1912). These determinations are neither naturalistic nor biological, being independent of anatomy though articulated with it, but are supported by the relational space created between mother and child, and are based on an identifying plot.

Secondly, we need to bear in mind that in these first moments— "before" access to the sexual difference—these imaginary identifications, masculine or feminine, coexist with a primordial, archaic feminine associated with the figure of the all-powerful, omnipotent mother. The primordial feminine is related to what is difficult to represent, what is beyond desire. It is about primary, pre-mirror experiences with kinaesthetic, sensorial characteristics that signal what is traumatic and wordless concerning these first experiences in the mother-child relationship.[3]

Both the mirror and the pre-mirror experiences promote the configuration of an ideal, pre-oedipal femininity. This encourages imaginary feminine identifications in the female and hinders the identifying process in the male, who must repress or sharply split off the pre-oedipal moments because they are linked to certain libidinal and bodily experiences related to the feminine/maternal permeation. *Thus the primordial feminine and gender diversity coexist.* We can only think in these terms, as we emphasized in the previous chapter, by applying theories of complexity which accept the heterogeneous and the coexistence of opposites; we also do so by using notions of coexisting temporalities in terms of significations and re-significations.

The pre-discourse and the symbolic

This coexistence between the primordial, archaic feminine and masculine/feminine gender diversity occurs in psychic spaces corresponding to the pre-oedipal field, usually considered a pre-symbolic or pre-discourse field. However, I would like to point out that the pre-oedipal field also contains a seed of symbolization. Winnicott (1959) developed the concept of a transitional space between mother and child, a space that involves creativity and symbolization. *Therefore, pre-discourse and an incipient core of symbolization coexist, even in contradiction, which allows us to think of the pre-oedipal space as a plural space.*

We consider that we cannot exclude femininity from the symbolic field and reduce it to an excluding, pre-discourse domain. This forces us to consider the multiplicity and plurality of its determinations. This implies that we need to think about *areas of overlapping and confluence*, about conjunction and disjunction, continuities and discontinuities organized between parental discourse and the child's psychic apparatus. It means thinking about the pre-oedipal space as a pre-symbolic space but also as an initiator of forms of symbolization. All this articulates with the oedipal resolution, in which thirdness motorizes the setting in motion of desire as well as the exogamic object-choice assumed by each subject.

As we proposed, the oedipal passage involves a *re-signification* of previous determinations, while interacting with *previous significations* mediated by maternal discourse. All these levels are articulated, but as we have seen, articulation does not imply symmetry between the sexes. *I consider that this discussion leaves open the question as to whether there is one symbolic law or a network of laws in the frame of processes which produce subjectivity.* We also need to examine in greater depth the core of symbolization inherent in the pre-oedipal phase.

About an additional psychic violence

For Aulagnier (1975), the mother's identifying enunciations anticipate the child's capacity to understand their meaning. They are conveyed by a primary, structuring and necessary violence. In my opinion, this statement should include an *additional psychic violence* which is the violence inherent in conceptions and mythologies concerning the assigned gender.

We consider the mother-child relational space a privileged area for displaying these categories. It is a space of localization, transmission and production of different forms of discourse concerning sexual difference which are an effect/product as well as producers/generators of knowledge about difference. Furthermore, these discourse productions and their silences act in a privileged way on the boy's or girl's body, making effects of truth, error or ignorance circulate regarding sexual difference. This means that through maternal discourse and care-giving an identifying path is established, based in turn on pre-existing significations. Our opinion is therefore that these identifying enunciations also affect gender identifications, both masculine and feminine. They are part of the ego as ideals, based on the narcissistic ideal ego-ego ideal line.

There is a psychic violence involved in assigning a sex at birth, being named as a boy or a girl, indicating a first loss: both sexes are no longer encompassed. This psychic violence is reproduced when access to sexual difference involves a loss dealt with the symbolic. Bisexuality and the androgynous are on this itinerary of narcissistic insistence and of phantasmatic completeness, in an attempt to resist incompleteness (Pontalis, 1982). Hermaphroditus and Salmacis incarnated the mythological wish to comprise both sexes. The punishment inflicted by the gods conceals and also reveals this wish. Virginia Woolf (1928) challenges the binary division of the sexes in her novel *Orlando*. The sex change operations of transsexuals express this mythological wish.

Belonging to one sex or the other implies incompleteness, first imaginary—even though narcissistic organization disavows it—and later on, dealing with the symbolic field. *However, we emphasize that the trajectory of desire is more complex than this masculine/feminine bipolarity. The movements of desire always go beyond the gender identity and also exceed the access to sexual difference.*

The structuring psychic violence of maternal discourse intersects with the violence of the third, paternal intervention. This violence is sustained by the imposition of renouncing the ability to comprise both sexes. In this sense, *for the psyche, any attack on narcissistic completeness is violence.* The intervention of the third party in the mother-child dyad implies recognition of a symbolic order transcending them and the loss of imaginary narcissistic completeness.[4] Thus the concept of thirdness, configured as a theoretical necessity, explains access to sexual difference in the frame of a given symbolic organization.

Representability of the feminine

It is also essential to consider some questions referring to a possible psychic representation of the feminine. We have pointed out that for Freud it is impossible to symbolize the feminine, the only feasible route being the phallic trajectory. The girl can only resolve her Oedipus complex by the penis = child equation, which means that she accesses femininity through maternity. This also implies that maternity would be only symbolic when it is phallic.

Our discussions need to include certain polarities situated in the line of the sexual difference. For Freud, and later for Lacan, the paths of femininity are travelled on the object's side of the road. We know that Freud (1923) proposes the subject/object dichotomy when he views the masculine/feminine categories. He articulates the masculine with the subject, the active and the possession of the penis, while the feminine remains related to the object, the passive and the vagina which lodges the penis. For Lacan (1972–73), the essential in the feminine position is to be the object of desire for a subject in a phallic position. This is Lacan's proposal in the "mathemes of sexuation" (1972–73), when he situates the subject, barred, on the side of the masculine position and the *object a*, the object cause of desire, on the side of the feminine position. However, although each man or woman can situate him- or herself in one of these places, thus indicating the individual's position, we cannot ignore, as Tort (1991) points out, *that the subjects who take up residence in these positions are already qualified as man or woman, which indicates a tautology.* This author thinks that the mathemes are the formal version of the subjection of women to the phantasm of masculine castration.

These positions are organized as discourse productions containing relations of power-domination, with effects on clinical phenomena. This leads us to a series of questions: Aside from the lack inherent in the structuring of the subject, is there a lack inherent in the feminine condition? In this case, does it refer to a lack of psychic representation of the feminine? If "the female sex has a character of absence, emptiness and hole, which makes it seem less desirable than the masculine sex, for what the latter offers as provocative" (Lacan,

1955–56), is this lack of symbolization structural in character? Does the impossible representation of silence, emptiness, lack and death find a vicarious road of representation in women? Is this road a short cut, or is it a short circuit, to avoid the castration anxiety referring to the male's threatened narcissism, by putting lack into an "outside"? In these terms, does the feminine offer, like an oxymoron,[5] representation for something that cannot be represented?

Knowledge and discourse concerning the sexual difference are structured between subject and object, active and passive, phallic and castrated, between what can and cannot be represented. When they are fastened onto masculine-feminine polarity, the obstacle generated needs to be dismantled. These polarities are points for the exercise of relations of force, which open up as options in the privileged space of sexuality (Foucault, 1984; Bourdieu, 1998). As we show in other chapters, these relations of power-knowledge may involve dimensions of domination or violence. When power is exercised as domination, the pure present established is then reproduced mechanically (Trías, 1983).

We note that in this relational structure the asymmetry of the sexes also implies a positioning connected with power. Love and desire relationships are a preferential expression of this display of effects of power that circulate among different types of enunciations. In this trajectory we find the masochistic position, sustained either by a man or by a woman. Accordingly, analytic work needs to aim towards the deconstruction of these identifying networks, in order to promote the generation of new meanings and psychic re-inscriptions in the context of genealogical research. It may open the way to reworking identifications and phantasms as well as illuminating psychic spaces which are difficult to represent. We need to develop our potential for questioning conceptions and mythologies which shape stereotypes of femininity and are conveyed as psychic violence—in the form of pre-existing signification—through parental discourse.

This process involves deconstructing the mandatory feature of the identifying project, as well as de-centring the initial project.[7] In the frame of symbolic re-processing—a task of mediation—the potential to break the One of the original project also develops. Thus a symbolic distance is created between each subject and his/her identifications. Therefore, when a subject removes the mark of the initial identifying project, which is not his or her own, a potential space is generated which allows the assumption of a singular project through cathexis and de-cathexis of representations. This process is defined by the subject's capacity to assume limits and incompleteness. It implies comprehending the assumption of subjectivity as a project, or as Kristeva (1986) puts it, subjectivity in process.

Notes

1. The infantile sexual theories are also shared by adults—men and women—and constitute an imaginary frame with powerful psychic effects, which should be deconstructed.
2. Cf. chapter 11, about the polysemic condition of the concept of difference. The precise relation between sexual difference and the linguistic or philosophical notions of difference, among other meanings, is not always properly specified.
3. For J. André (1995) there is an early femininity for both sexes, which he conceptualizes with the theory of seduction, as intrusion, fracture and breaking in of adult sexuality. He maintains that early femininity is not equivalent to knowledge of the vagina. He bases his thesis on the theory of the cloaca which is also an erogenous zone for the girl.
4. This third party transcends the father figure, since it can also be located in the mother figure. It involves cultural symbolic mediation in the field of intersubjectivity.
5. We apply the concept of oxymoron—a rhetorical figure which attributes the opposite meaning to something—as a contribution to forms of complex thought that go beyond a radical binary system and differ from classical oppositions and schematic polarities.
6. Baranger's notion of dis-identification refers to this process (1989).

CHAPTER THREE

At the limits of the feminine:
the Other

It is a challenge for psychoanalysts to consider the category of "woman" in psychoanalysis. First of all this requires a conceptual delimitation. What relation is there between women and the feminine? How do these terms relate to femininity and female sexuality? Are any formal categories that encompass the question of the sexual difference without any historical or trans-subjective connections? And at the same time: what is specific to psychoanalysis in this topic? We also need a careful analysis of the conceptual categories, myths and beliefs on the female condition that psychoanalysis shares with other types of thinking. This means deciphering the unexpressed representational background behind theoretical discourse and organized systems of thought. It also involves including the conjectural bias inherent in all theories. This search must consider the complex relation between the subject who elaborates the theory and the accepted discourse on the sexual difference. It also involves understanding how the psychic apparatus categorizes the sexual difference.

With no pretensions to offering absolute or definitive solutions to these questions, I will discuss the concept of crisis, focusing mainly on certain conceptions regarding women and the feminine. I will try to draw a comparison between the crisis of conceptions about woman in contemporary thinking—a crisis in the sense of mobility resulting from the breakdown of fixed meanings—and the moments of crisis occurring in the course of life for all women (adolescence and the intermediate and advanced stages of adulthood). At these moments, former crises are expressed retroactively, questions arise concerning the feminine position, and eventually possibilities for the production of new meanings may also emerge.

I am referring to crises as narcissistic de-centring and as the rupture of a continuity (Kaes, 1979); as the loss of references and codes, with no alternative replacement codes. Crises are optimal moments for the mobilization of beliefs, ideals and representations once considered immutable. Not only individual ideals: also the perennial conceptions that support the philosophical, religious and cultural discourses on women. In this context, I conceptualize crises as the place of contradictions and antagonisms between divergent proposals on femininity, moments which question the foundations and fixed view of the world.

Psychoanalytic discourse should not escape this critical mobilization. We know that the theories about women oscillate between two extremes. On the one hand they consider women as the wordless, as belonging to the field of Nature, bodies and emotions; they therefore add to women the condition of enigmatic. At the other extreme, other theories consider that there would be no woman outside the symbolic field; however, in this case they face an additional difficulty: how to theorize the sexual difference beyond the phallic-castrated opposition. We also need to bear in mind that when we speak of what is "natural", we are referring to a representational field concerning Nature. Language creates a space of intermediation, so that the "real nature" of the human subject, man or woman, is "re-produced" (Lorite Mena, 1987).

Freud and Women

The works of Freud are extremely complex in regard to theories about women and sexual difference. Freudian theory retains its freshness because it is not unitary, even though Freud never explicitly abandons a positivist notion of science. He straddles positivism and the notion of the unconscious, which questions any totally rational attempt to understand the subject.[1] On the one hand his ideas about the Oedipus and castration complexes are de-centred from any biological conception of sexual difference, since the difference is not exclusively in the order of the biological, but rather part of a chain of significations. The same is true for the Freudian conception of the complemental series (1916–17), whose complexity (constitutional background, childhood experiences and accidental adult experiences) is contrary to the univocal character of the biological, and thus becomes part of a plural organization. Psychoanalytic access to sexual difference is a symbolic operation, an operation of culture.

But Freud himself reveals that his opinions are inevitably nourished by a masculine view when he refers to the riddle of the nature of femininity. He says (1933): "Nor will you have escaped worrying over this problem, those of you who are men; to those of you who are women this will not apply, you are yourselves the problem." Freud read Schopenhauer as well as Rousseau (1933), who maintained that the search for abstract and speculative ideas, scientific principles and axioms, everything that tends to generalization, is out of the woman's reach. In the same vein, we see that Freud (1933) considers that a woman aged thirty "often frightens us by her psychical rigidity and unchangeability". That is to say a person with such mental rigidity that she would lack any possibility of psychic mobility; a definitive position of the libido, as if "the difficult development to femininity had exhausted the possibilities of the person concerned" (Freud, 1933). According to Freud, this marks women's "precariousness" as social beings. For this reason, he affirms that their potential for development in the field of reason depends on their masculine components. This idea is supported by a heavy theoretical postulate in the libidinal field: the girl is a "little boy" in her pre-oedipal stage. And the road to femininity is a series of successive shifts from the mother to the father, from the penis to the child, in which the maximum goal of femininity is maternity which, paradoxically, is an aim in the phallic order (Freud, 1925, 1932).

In another perspective, we have seen that Lacan (1972–73) conceptualizes the feminine position as contingent and singular, he denies it as a universal category. These formalizations state that the category of woman, as "not all", is not subject to the universal condition of castration, her relation to castration being defined individually, and always in relation to the phallic function. His proposal on female *jouissance*, as a supplement exceeding phallic *jouissance*, supported by the order of the Real, implies a non-complementary relation between the sexes and can be seen as an attempt to de-centre the strict phallic logic. Although for Lacan the woman as an *object a* is situated at the meeting point of the three orders—the Real, the Symbolic and the Imaginary—the emphasis he places on feminine *jouissance*, linked to mystical *jouissance*, tending towards the infinite, involves the risk of shifting women ultimately into exclusion from the symbolic.

The feminine in crisis: the intermediate stages of life

Our starting point is situations of crisis, with an emphasis on the crises of the intermediate ages in women. Those situations enlighten conceptions, beliefs and unconscious fantasies in relation to the feminine position. Former crises are re-signified, ideals falter—on the vector of the narcissistic ideal ego/ego ideal—identifications are mobilized or break down, the position in regard to sexual desire is thrown into play. This occurs in the frame of a reactivation of the Oedipus complex and of mourning for lost or unaccomplished ideals. These crises reveal fissures, created by the fall of an imaginary vision of the self and the world, which ultimately open the possibility for questioning fixed meanings.

In these movements of order-disorder, myths are attempts to organize chaos (Balandier, 1988). I consider that this mythical organization has a structuring character which provides meaning but also organizes a vision of the world and of genders which can be presented imaginarily as being immutable. We must also remember that these situations of individual crisis—which acquire a more specific category as life expectancy is prolonged—occur in the frame of a crisis of cultural symbolic references. The crisis of binary proposals on the sexual difference, as well as the androgynous condition and transsexualism, expresses anxiety in regard to the uncertainties of sexuality. In turn, these lead to a defensive reinforcement of a rigid and a-historic binary opposition, as a resource of the discourse. That is to say a complex intertwining occurs between crises on an individual level and the theoretical developments related to the feminine position. One aspect emerging from the crises of the intermediate years of life is the confrontation with a limited temporality. The contradiction between the immortal time of narcissism and a limited temporality comes forward with force, and the preconscious insists on it.

Jacques (1978) describes the emergence of depressive types of crisis with hypochondriac fears, which demand the working through of mourning for lost youth as well as of hate and ambivalence. He develops the concept of "sculpted creativity" as a process of change in the way of working, in quality and contents; a project in the face of a crisis. However, he refers to the masculine condition without considering what specifically concerns the feminine condition.

But why discuss these crises in relation to the feminine? After all, men also have a body and go through the crises of middle age. However, the masculine and the feminine positions are structured differently in relation to sexual desire, beauty and *jouissance*. This is a differential position which responds neither to a masculine nor to a feminine essence but is relational and connected within a synchronic-diachronic context.

The abrupt fall of identifying references and the ideals adhering to them is the terrain on which anxiety re-emerges. This underscores an especially interesting point, since at those times the threat consists of the return of what was idealized and ominous in early times. These aspects, affected by splitting, are updated in a specific way in the middle-aged woman. At these stages "the horror of the ominous" emerges with special force; it may be experienced equally by either sex, but is located in women by displacement. Our idea in discussing these moments is to emphasize a particular type of confrontation with the traumatic or with a representational void. It is noteworthy that in this situation the representational void is superimposed on the existential void, and as an escape route it can become an anchor point for extreme idealizations or for denigration of women.

We know that historically there have been no rites of passage for women traversing these stages as there are for other vital moments in the life of men and women such as birth, circumcision or wedding (Bart, 1979). This gives them an unnamed character, connected with the theories about women based on a wordless condition of the feminine. Women appear as disquieting "others", which can lead us to interpret difference in terms of inequality or to exclude them from the symbolic field. In this sense the archetypical figure of the witch can be seen as an attempt—beyond any other valid interpretation—to give symbolization to or shape out something which is felt to be uncanny in order to put a limit on the anxiety it provokes.

The beautiful and the form

Women have for centuries been the expression of the beautiful and of seduction; form and woman have been and are still terms of an apparently indissoluble equation. The notion of "formativity" is a reference to the way the subject places him- or herself in relation to the world, resolving this attitude on the level of structures with a "way of forming" (Eco, 1979). This aims at certain formative tendencies present in a given culture and period, just as investigations on the structures of forms have shown, in Eco's references to Luigi Pareyson's *Aesthetics*.

But the beautiful is the form that conceals the form-less, the disquieting and the threatening: a source of anxiety. On the one hand the form-less is an expression of decadence and deterioration, but on the other hand it also expresses what is excluded from the symbolic field. In this sense, what is more form-less than the nearly wordless quality of the primary mother-child experience? This uncanny side of incestuous *jouissance* is split off in both sexes but returns, placed in women, because they represent the maternal double, with no fissures in the imaginary realm.

I consider that what is split off in these conditions is *the feminine*, an expression of the primary experience in relation to the maternal. *Thus the feminine is a notion shared by both sexes, but by a shift of categories it is placed in women.* In this perspective the feminine implies no confrontation with incompleteness. But why call it the feminine when it is a category inherent in both sexes? Basically because *it incarnates aspects of the initial mother-infant relationship which are transferred, by analogy and through discourse, onto women.* This is related to fusion and to the equation of two different categories: woman and mother, which have a necessary connection but are nonetheless not equal. Thus *a basic misunderstanding is established, by which women now incarnate what is wordless, linked to the archaic primordial stages of life.* It is in this context of equation that we must place Freud's declaration (1933) that "even a marriage is not made secure until the wife has succeeded in making her husband her child as well, and in acting as a mother to him."

Kristeva developed the concept of *chora* to express precisely the idea of the feminine as what cannot be symbolized in reference to those primary moments. For this author, this archaic dimension lies in the category of the Other, and therefore exerts a disruptive influence on subjectivity, since it is not totally split off from the symbolic (Moi, 1986). We underscore that the Other can be interpreted from different perspectives: on the one hand it seems to be what can be discarded or excluded from the fabric of the symbolic, while on the other hand, in its position of eccentricity, it questions the power of the centre and the certainties of absolute Reason.

The popularity of plastic surgery and the attempt to attain eternal youth are part of a project to recover definition through form. In this oscillation between the definite and the indefinite, the form *versus* the formless, we include the fantasy, rooted in narcissism, of the power to give form. The active creation of form in this case is a defensive aspect in the face of the "horror", the traumatic effect of incestuous *jouissance* which, as we said, is transferred to women by making them equivalent to the archaic mother.[2]

Sexual desire

We must also remark that the woman-mother equation may hinder the question of sexual desire in women, in the sense that their desire would thereby focus on the child. In this way sexual desire would be included in a phallic logic, based on a knowledge rooted in a certain sexual order. In this perspective, if feminine sexual desire is not complementary or identical to masculine desire, a disorder is created by its differential non-phallic character (Lorite Mena, 1987).

But what happens to sexual desire in the process of aging? The fall of the aesthetic ideals and the problem of being less desirable are in the order of narcissistic wounds. According to Sobchak (1994), sexual desire becomes inappropriate and transgressive. For this author, make-up therefore represents the desire for youth, beauty and seduction, and is one of the ways to be reminded of sexual desire. But make-up also reveals fear of the inscription of a caricature of the subject's own sexual desire, and of all that once was desirable.

Kristeva (1980) discusses the phenomenon of abjection and its relation to horror: the abject, before the object, is at the limits of the thinkable and the assimilable, and confronts us with our most primitive attempts to differentiate ourselves from the maternal entity. It also represents the division between an invisible interior and a visible, decadent exterior. This is related to the association between the abject part and the body in its decadence, which falls upon the archaic mother, represented by women.

Thus the fear of aging is displaced and localized in women, a fear of mortality and physical aging. Women also tend to take upon themselves the abject part related to the body and its decadence. In the imaginary, this can be presented in the form of decadent bodies that approach a man, who recoils in horror. These figures are related to death and to the unspeakable rather than to sexual desire and castration anxiety. It is no coincidence that the Fates (Death) are presented as women and that the idea of one's own death is featured as something destructive, hostile, sinister. When they appear as images of horror, these representations also evidence the hostility of women produced by the double standard regarding aging—dependent on the person's sex—proposed by the trans-individual discourse (Sobchak, 1994).

We consider that these figures refer to the ominous: the *Unheimlich* supports semantic ambiguity by denoting what is familiar as well (Freud, 1919). They allude to primordial moments, to an excess of excitation of an incestuous order, to the familiar and homely, which becomes ominous; to all that inspires anxiety and also hostility and violence, directed ultimately towards the pre-oedipal mother. These experiences correlate with the absolute and idealized character assigned to the maternal condition. Thus we emphasize that incestuous, archaic *jouissance* is supported for both sexes by a pre-symbolic, pre-oedipal field; but there is splitting and displacement by which it is localized in women as uncanny femininity. Is this movement related, in masculine fantasies, to the threat of being trapped in a dual relation with the all-powerful mother, including the consequent attack on his masculinity? In this way the female condition would imaginarily support the "idealness and uncanniness" of the initial experiences, since both sexes localize them in women.

As we have said, the proposals of medical technology tend to neutralize these figures referring to the ominous, and are equally an extreme attempt to throw out finitude. Also, just as W. Benjamin (1989) affirms with respect to the serial reproduction of works of art (nobody knows which the original one is), plastic surgeries propose a model, always the same one, which is reproduced, with the consequent loss of the original individuality: a technologically manipulated, perfectible body whose model could be a clone. In this sense everything could be replaced and also discarded. This phenomenon is related to Baudrillard's (1990) thesis concerning the "aesthetization" of everyday life, the pure circulation of images forming the "trans-aesthetics of banality".

It is precisely the mobility of crises that, by definition, assists us in reviewing these categories. Crises as moments when historical sequence is broken, but also providing the possibility to historically construct, to break up the cycle of repetitions, both in theory as well as in the life of each subject. That is to say crisis as the decisive moment between progression and regression, order and disorder, de-structuring and restructuring. Crises also point to the capacity of the psyche to generate new representational contents and to a potential for the eventual recovery of barely symbolized elements at the same time, bearing in mind that, as Guillaumin (1979) points out, there is a non-symbolized or not yet symbolized base that guarantees and supports symbolic development. This base, he says, is the mother's breast.

The limit

The feminine always appears as a problem of the limits, of the margins. To speak of margins usually involves speaking of the excluded, of what cannot be symbolized. We also know that it is at the limits that a theory is put to the test and that its centre is the most immobile and least questionable part; that it is in the nuclei of theories where the violence of adhesion to certain parameters is expressed, revealing the strength in each analyst of his or her analytic and theoretical history, filiations and everything that is assumed and implicit.

However, the view from the edge allows us to consider everything that a particular theory excludes—since if the parameters never change, nor does our view—and to reveal theoretical paradoxes and their effects in clinical work. That is, on the one hand the limits mean exclusion, while on the other hand they aim to disassemble and deconstruct rigidly unifying concepts, in the sense of questioning certainties, absolute knowledge, extreme rationalism and the rejection of diversity. This is highly important for the analysis of concep-tions on women and the feminine, conceptions which lie at the foundations of the psychoanalytic theory and are inexorably expressed in clinical work.

Our intention is to return to the concept of margin, edge or limit, and to work on it in relation to the feminine. As we mentioned before, Trías (1991) conceptualizes the limit as a logical category, comparing it to the areas of territory left in the wake of the advance of the Roman armies, between Roman territory and the territory of the conquered peoples. There was a triple boundary: one's own world, the foreign world and the *limes* or frontier boundary. The latter was a zone of confluence, a different, heterogeneous area, where laws and phenomena differing from the original ones were created.

The concepts on women and the feminine emerged in the interstices of knowledge of Modernity as a site of enigmas, the "dark continent", a mysterious place concerning that knowledge. In this sense the limit points to the character of otherness assigned to the feminine. However, beyond its negative or enigmatic character, we can view the concept of limit as a space with its own laws, which thus emphasizes its positive condition. Continuing in this line, we can also consider that between the child and the mother there is a limit area, a space of intermediation and processing of meanings concerning the sexual difference, generated by the mother's discourse. We mentioned that Freud (1933 [1932]) held that "a mother is only brought unlimited satisfaction by her relation to a son; this is altogether the most perfect, the most free of ambivalence of all human relationships." We also recall that Aulagnier (1975) points out that "being a girl or a boy is the first discovery of the ego in the field of identifying references." From the beginning, this leaves a gender mark that precedes the access to sexual difference, which in turn each subject symbolizes in a singular manner. This is to say that there is a history of identifications which intersects with a history of the ideas and ideals in regard to the feminine, forming a weave that must be undone. This alludes to original imaginary representations that lead to an incipient psychic organization which at that moment had a structuring function.

There is an intersection between the common discourse, with its myths, fables and beliefs about women and the feminine, and the singularity of each history; between individual unconscious phantasm and collective constructions. In this perspective, we consider that the foundational encounter, on the plane of inter-subjectivity, refers to the Other not only as a provider of signifiers but inevitably as a source of significations. If we attempt to think about the feminine in this way, we can think in terms of a notion where complexity governs, where heterogeneous logics co-exist; a field that questions the certainties of the centre, which pushes, tenses and interrogates. This co-existence does not imply any kind of theoretical relativism, but an opening to find ways of thinking which, as we have proposed, can accept divergences and the co-existence of opposites. I am referring to logic categories which allow us to think in terms of simultaneity and antagonism, and therefore also permit a different vision of notions undergoing a process of critical revision as the feminine position: *limit-spaces*, where *the feminine*—not the woman— is seen as a metaphoric incarnation, as a hinge between the original (the archaic) and the symbolic field. We also need to stress that the archaic is supported in turn by an oscillation between idealization/ fascination and the ominous/threatening.

These limit-spaces are areas of conjunction-disjunction between the parental unconscious and the child's unconscious, between the imaginary and the symbolic, the ideal ego and the ego ideal, the social imaginary and the individual imaginary, between sexual desire and *jouissance*, between trans-subjective determinations and the oedipal process in each subject. These are spaces where nature is not natural, where phallic logic is constantly surpassed. In this frame, a salient point is that the feminine position is configured in a space which is necessarily asymmetric in relation to the masculine position. One of the roots of this asymmetry responds to the parental discourse and desires which, coupled with the infant's own drive activity, place boys and girls in different positions in relation to sexual desire, love and *jouissance*.

Otherness

The feminine has always incarnated the category of otherness: not only in the most obvious sense of an imaginary and inferior alter ego but, as Levinas (1947) describes it, as mystery. This is a mystery which, like death, acquires the character of absolute otherness. He says: "The Other as an Other is not only an alter ego: it is what I am not . . . The setback that allows one term to keep its otherness absolutely is the feminine." For Levinas, the feminine is essentially the Other, not as an object or as the notion of the unknown or ignored woman, but as a category that "retires into its mystery", and cannot be translated into terms of power. He emphasizes that in the evocation of sexuality, because of a certain mistake, it has been attached to the humanity of women. However, Levinas postulates a strong equivalence between the feminine and otherness, which will be analysed in this text.

From another perspective, the margins point to the character of otherness assigned to the feminine, on the basis that in androcentric cultures it incarnates the Other, everything that does not fit into the canons of the norm. Since the concept of woman as the Other of the norm is rooted in philosophy, religions and social discourse, it is perhaps excessively ambitious for psychoanalysis to posit that its hypotheses on the sexual difference be exempt from the proposals and conventions that infiltrate the weave of culture. Kristeva (1988) maintains that in the Judeo-Christian cultures, based on a patriarchal order, women are seen as the Other of the symbolic, of the law-of-the-father. *In this view, the character of otherness does not point to any a-historic essence of the feminine.* So if we consider the feminine in its condition of otherness as a historical version or incarnation of the wordless, primary incestuous *jouissance*, related to the first mother-child relationship, the process of shifting by which it comes to represent the sexual difference is of the utmost importance. In this way the enigma of the sexual difference overlaps with the enigma of the origins, and both become incarnated in women. That is, *the enigma of sexuality becomes the enigma of femininity.* This adherence has heavy theoretical and clinical consequences.

Kristeva (1988) postulates a paradox for women: either they identify with the mother and are left outside the symbolic, or they identify with the father and thereby support the patriarchal structure, and need to negate their feminine ego. This extreme dilemma leads us to the question concerning the given, immutable relation between the law-of-the-father, the symbolic and the representational field. This relates to the strict binary splitting between symbolic paternity in the social field and maternity with deep roots in the real, which in a certain sense is superimposed on the "natural order". The overlapping of the symbolic third party function with paternity—which habitually represents it—can lead to certain theoretical extremes which place women in a *jouissance* without law, in opposition to men, situated predominantly in the field of the law. Furthermore, if the difference is placed exclusively in the body or in pleasure as inherent in women, this encourages representational exclusion. How can we therefore interconnect these fields without excluding women from the symbolic, and also avoid falling into the hegemony of a law without *jouissance*? This also leads us to question whether the field of the feminine *is* the non-symbolized or whether it incarnates the non-symbolized in relation to *one* version of the norm. Assoun (1993) points out that the feminine challenges the symbolic: a conception different from being excluded from the symbolic field. The question of the feminine and women is also connected with a broader problem: how to categorize a field beyond the symbolic. What is it that the omnipresence of the symbolic would leave out? When he discusses this problem, Deleuze (1995) sustains a perception of reality previous to language which is not simplified by the intervention of language.

Paradoxes of feminine subjectivity

The problems of sexual difference point to the way each subject appropriates the pre-subjective and trans-subjective determinations and how he or she inscribes the difference itself symbolically. That is to say how subjects relate to the sex they belong to with organizing meaning. This is a complex operation, always incomplete and problematic, which also signals the need to accept the heterogeneous, the antagonistic, and to grasp all the determinations at work, however difficult it may be to integrate them theoretically. It involves, as we have said, recognizing divergent domains which support the feminine position: *femininity* in the field of identifications concerning gender ideals, *female sexuality* in the order of sexual desire and choice of object, and *the feminine/maternal* in the field of the archaic, the maternal, inherent in both sexes. It also assumes the recognition of areas of conjunction-disjunction between them. And yet these limits cannot save us from unavoidable ambiguity and eventual shifts in the use of these terms.

Access to difference, as a symbolic operation, involves recognition of otherness. This excludes the existence of a pre-existing All, as well as that of a duality involving fusion into a One. Levinas (1947) says: "Failure of communication in love constitutes precisely the positivity in the relationship: the absence of the Other is precisely its presence as an Other".

At this point we emphasize that the Other, in relation to the feminine, is polysemic and multi-determining. On the one hand, the character of otherness is rooted in a configuration of the social discourse in which the Other is women; on the other hand, in the construction of subjectivity, the Other is the archaic, the maternal, what was once familiar and homely and has become foreign and hostile, and as such has been split off from the symbolic weave. This will be transferred and localized in women as mystery or enigma. Thus women appear as the Other for men, but as a displacement of the maternal—the archaic—that is the Other for both sexes. It is from the origin that the Other, meaning what is strange, is constructed.

Every subject, man or woman, is confronted with otherness, but women redundantly also incarnate it. This creates a paradox, since if the feminine appears to be the metaphor of otherness and this in turn is incarnated in women, how can they accept their subjectivity on the basis of the overlapping condition of otherness and "objectness"? This paradox is seated, as we have seen, on the shifts, overlapping and equations between the feminine, female sexuality, femininity, women and the condition of otherness.

So how can we think about feminine subjectivity in the midst of these snares of mirror identity, equation with the Other and symbolic omnidetermination? We consider that although there is no feminine subjectivity outside the symbolic, this subjectivity is nonetheless not defined simply by its relation to the signifying weave. If we add to this the structuring power, not just illusory or deceitful, of the imaginary order, and the character of otherness which pressures from the split-off maternal archaic elements as well as from the constructions of culture, the result forms a dynamic, multidimensional field.

***

In this chapter, I begin by using the concept of crisis to help us think about the movements and questions surrounding the conceptualizations of the feminine and women in psychoanalysis. I have chosen the crises of the middle years in women, since at that stage certain aspects in relation to the ominous and the Other emerge with particular clarity. Beauty, as a form, structures a configuration that tends to split off and reject these upsetting, hostile aspects.

The feminine condition has always incarnated a place of otherness. In this respect, I have tried to differentiate a double root. On the one hand there is the Other as the foreign, the hostile and split off in the primary mother-child relationship, what was once familiar and homely, now become ominous. *As long as the mother continues to be the primary other, this configures the concept of "the feminine/maternal" inherent in both sexes.* In this context the feminine appears as an extension of the mother's gender. Thus, through complex displacements, the maternal is named the feminine, and the archaic, the maternal. This field—the archaic—generates the character of enigma or mystery which this movement of displacement localizes in women. On the other hand, the condition of otherness is not exempt from the determinations proposed by the current notions on sexual difference. It is this double determination that supports the equations woman-mother and feminine-woman: equations which need to be undone, while bearing in mind that we will also need to integrate the inevitable relations between these terms.

At the same time I postulate that the Other is conceptualized in relation to the limit or the margins. This produces a marginal or centrifugal character on the one hand; but on the other hand, the concept of limit is emphasized as a space with its own laws. From the limits the knowledge of the centre is questioned, and from the Other the certainties about oneself vacillate.

I have also emphasized that *the feminine*, considered as the maternal/archaic, as the Other for both sexes, is heterogeneous to the order of sexual desire (*female sexuality*) and to the field of gender identifications (*femininity*). These fields are neither axiomatic nor a-historical. This implies ongoing multidimensional structuring in which no component by itself can encompass the questions and issues involved, and which can only be defined in terms of complexity and simultaneity.

Notes

1. The notion of unconscious is tied to the ideas developed by German Romanticism in the 19th century, which influenced Freud.
2. Cf. Chapter Seven for other theoretical perspectives concerning maternity.

CHAPTER FOUR

The feminine in the middle stages of life: the efficacy of an imaginary

We are aware of the impact of the passing of time on anyone, whether a man or a woman, and we also know that it involves facing a dark and unknown side of our psyche. At these moments we question ideals and values, anxieties and fears appear or resurface, and depression may set in. The imaginary which once provided security fails us, and the threat of aging and deterioration emerges.

In this context we emphasize that the concepts of youth, adulthood and old age are constantly being modified. They are subject to re-definition time and again, while chronological limits and stages fade out. Prolonged life expectancy in recent decades is creating an increasingly important area which exerts increasing weight as a turning point between maturity and old age. We are not referring to the so-called crisis of adult life, which is a crisis with a prospective, questioning character, when projects are re-confirmed or redefined. We refer to the crises of the intermediate years of a woman's life, whose scope is broader than the concept of menopause, with its medical resonances. They are often triggered by menopause or the departure of children, and are sometimes accentuated by the absence of alternative projects. They may take the form of feelings of emptiness, failure or decadence, or may be expressed by somatizations, hypomania, depression or states of panic.

The confrontation with biological laws, the sureness of death, aging and the consequent narcissistic affront are inevitable. But one issue we need to emphasize is the woman's feeling of her own decadence: the loss of physical beauty, since the aesthetic aspect is traditionally one of the strong points of femininity. These moments have a traumatic impact which can set off mechanisms of repetition or also open opportunities for change and transformation. A psychic space opens between rupture and continuity. This moment of temporal intersection between past history (including the more or less successful resolution of former crises) and the present holds potential for facing the future.

We also point out that there is a tendency to frame the discourse on femininity in the context of Western societies. In spite of great social mobility in this century, when many conceptions in relation to women have been modified, these changes do not affect the different social strata and different ethnic and religious groups in the same way, thus reinforcing the need to narrow our discourse.

Although the crises of middle age affect both men and women, it is important to stress that in women the relation between the passing of time and the marks on the body is very specific, and these variables are not disconnected from the ideals proposed and sustained by culture in regard to femininity. This requires us to reflect on certain figures which shape the feminine mythically, especially with reference to the middle stages of life, in relation to feminine ideals and their vicissitudes.

Continuing the discussions in the previous chapter, I will now take up one aspect of these issues, viewing these stages of middle age in women as a psychic space where individual ideals of femininity undergo a crisis. However, I consider that this inevitably involves collective ideals and the social imaginary with its conceptions about women. The intersection between these two fields creates tensions because of the eventual opposition between collective and individual ideals, which may lead to identification conflicts. To this panorama we add the ongoing reformulation of both historical and individual ideals, while at the same time former conceptions persist and thus may come into conflict with what is new. The coexisting mobility and inertia create a specific field. *Between the individual and collective ideals on the one hand and the present and past ideals on the other, complex networks of articulation and opposition are created.* These are areas of intermediation between an inside and an outside, between social discourse and the individual psyche. These intersections are evidence of the contradictions and paradoxes that the feminine reveals in the theory. They are spaces of intermediation which are embodied in the psyche through the system of ideals, formed in the ideal ego/ego ideal line and ultimately incarnated in identifications. In this line we include the absolute, omnipotent ideals of infancy as well as the well-pruned ideals delimited by symbolic elaboration.

History of women?

The question has often been asked whether there is a history of women, and even whether women can speak for themselves (Duby & Perrot, 1990). This point alludes to an ancestral conception by which the rational corresponds to men and the emotional to women, coinciding with the opposition between culture and nature. The idea of women as weak, incomplete and inferior beings, or embodying demonic temptation, runs through the centuries and is evidenced in religious, philosophical and medical discourses, myths and customs. We see it in Talmudic conceptions of women as sorceresses and depositories of a dangerous sexuality. It is widely known that up to the Council of Trent, women were not considered to have a soul. In some primitive peoples, menstruating women were excluded because of their supposedly evil influence. In others, there were ceremonies in which women were burned alive with their dead husbands.

Israel (1979) describes the American Indian legend of the "tooth-filled vaginas" which come out at harvest-time and, when captured by the men, are divested of their teeth, returned to their place and fastened by the clitoral nail. For this author, this legend translates a phantasy related to fear of women which recalls the ablation of the clitoris performed on pre-pubertal Muslim girls, among other rationales as a way of controlling their sexual enjoyment.

Nineteenth century medical knowledge justified female inferiority. Bouillaud, using an analogical type of thinking, maintained that the uterus was not an essential organ in women because it did not exist in men. Erasmus (1511), in *The Praise of Folly*, considered women as stupid and mad animals, while Plato hesitated whether to include them in the ranks of rational animals or with the beasts. These hesitations were the same as Freud's (1933) when he described female characteristics on an empirical level: little sense of justice, weaker social interests and less aptitude for sublimation.

From this brief review we see that if there were a history of women it would be a history "in negative". We find, inside the cracks which appear in the positive histories, a guiding thread of silences and empty spaces that we need to decipher and write about.

The ideals and the void

In the middle stages of life, the problems connected to femininity in the history of each woman are brought into the present. Diverse moments, logical or chronological, may trigger this confrontation.

We know that certain ideals of femininity (and also of masculinity) are part of an imaginary shared by men and women. We also define these ideals as systems of beliefs with extraordinary structuring power, and insist that the theory is not immune to these powerful influences. Some of these ideals nail being a woman to essentialist parameters which represent two opposing conceptions. On the one hand there is idealization and over-sizing in connection with the figures of the Mother and the Virgin, associated with purity, emotions, sensitivity, love and beauty. On the other hand we see its nether side, repudiation in connection with the figures of the prostitute, sexual temptation, the demonic and the horrifying. Some of these figures can also become a condition of love (Freud, 1910). In this context one of the strong proposals in relation to femininity is maternity. We note that maternity involves a desire-drive circuit, as well as love and its narcissistic components; therefore, it is no longer just a natural or biological fact for women but indicates a confrontation with their conflicts and sexual desire.

In the intermediate stages of life, the de-centring of the maternal place as a representational support, with reinforcement of the con-comitant drive intensity (Freud, 1937), can be experienced as facing emptiness. Maternity offers positive ideals in relation to the search for psychic representation. In this sense the crisis of the maternal ideals involves an identification conflict in whose interstices we find silence, as an exclusion from a symbolic field. At this crossroads the relations between repetitive time and irreversible time are updated, and every woman either re-defines, consciously or unconsciously, a project concerning identifications and desire, or alternatively suffers the "fate of a disposable object".

The reverse of the ideals, the witch and the uncanny

One figure embodying this fate is the witch. We know that witches were women who devoted themselves to curing illness and that they met in *sabbats*; since they departed from the accepted canons, they were considered heretics and ended up being burned at the stake (Israel, 1979). They were accused of meeting illegally, of pacts with the devil, of copulating with *incubi* and *succubi*, of destroying crops and stealing children. For Harris (1974), even though they were harmless, they were persecuted as being responsible for the injustices of their age and for spreading the energies of protest against corruption of the secular and ecclesiastical powers.

However, it is interesting to ask why these witches, as defined above, were women, since we know that the wizard or sorcerer was the respected wise man who was never persecuted. This is related to a peculiar intertwining: on the one hand the condemnation by the Church of pagan practices associated with the demonic, and on the other the misogyny which since the classical age had considered women as demonic creatures in relation to sexual desire and temptation, based on a sinful conception of sexuality.

One wonders also why they were generally old. They were usually poor peasants who, if they did not marry or enter a convent, or were widowed, found no place or future and became suspicious. Many were midwives or healers, and were persecuted together with the Moorish and Jewish healers. Old women in the Middle Ages only kept their place if they were part of a household as a unit of production and consumption. Otherwise they could fall into the category of witches because of their loss of beauty and capacity to procreate, because of their use of sexuality outside the prescribed conditions, or because of their autonomous activity as healers (Saez, 1979). Thus the threat was to become a "disposable object".

Also of interest are the studies of certain horror films ("The Wasp Woman", "The Leech Woman"), where the main character is usually a greying, middle-aged woman, alone and disdained by men, oppressed by the fear of becoming invisible to them and therefore isolated sexually. Through a metamorphosis she becomes a vengeful, horrifying and cruel being (Sobchak, 1994): there is a transformation from a frightened woman into a woman who is frightening, in the form of a decadent body which threatens a man, who recoils in terror. This represents the horror of aging in a culture which puts its money on immortality and beauty, locating this horror in the woman who has lost these attributes.

An important point to highlight in this sense is that the feminine is associated with a very special relationship with the body. A woman's life involves a series of physical marks (the menarche, pregnancies, deliveries and menopause) which indicate times, sequences and ruptures that remove her quite early from the possibility of a corporeal abstraction which is generally more associated with the masculine condition. Since the different forms of discourse on femininity have always accentuated a high narcissistic component, the danger of deterioration can become a lethal threat to her narcissistic ego. In women, this is even greater if devalued ideals concerning femininity are actualized. We are referring not only to the biological body but also to the erogenous, libidinal body; and also to a body whose silences place her erogenous condition in suspension. This relates to another situation which we often observe: the amazement, anxiety and even feelings of threat experienced by women in the middle stages of life if they notice rejected aspects of their mother in themselves (Freud, 1931). Thus what is familiar becomes uncanny, foreign and hostile (Freud, 1919).

From this perspective, the figure of the witch builds a story embodying sinister aspects of the primordial moments related to the mother-child bond which press to get closer, both in men and in women, in the intermediate stages of life. In this way we see how categories which are hard to represent are actualized in connection with primordial moments of an incestuous type. These categories are localized in women, and thus they acquire a figure. The psychic apparatus attempts to fence in, surround and symbolize them in each of these updatings.

The "repudiation of femininity"

In "The Taboo of Virginity" (1918), Freud points out that men are afraid of being weakened by women, infected with their femininity, and consequently showing their impotence. He adds that the precepts of avoidance express a basic horror of women. The feminine appears as being something strange, incomprehensible and therefore hostile. In another text, "Analysis Terminable and Interminable" (1937), he maintains that in both sexes there is a "repudiation of femininity". And could the "horror of the female genitals" involve a paradoxical position for men, since they should desire what is "least desirable"? Or, on the contrary, would the "horror" provide narcissistic reassurance in the face of "consummated castration" and its concomitant anxiety?

For Kristeva (1988), the rejection of the feminine is based on the presentation of the feminine as something strange or foreign in relation to a norm, the masculine. She points out that this uncanny strangeness expresses the fascinated rejection of the Other that lies in the heart of "ourselves": the Other of death, the Other of women, the Other of the indomitable drive.

As we said in the previous chapter, we need to underscore that the anxiety related to the mysterious dimension of sexual difference is displaced onto the feminine, characterized as otherness. Another aspect to highlight is that the decadence of physical beauty can lead to the condition of "disposable object", which ties in with certain aspects of so-called postmodernity, where everything is rapidly disposable: theories, ideas, information and also persons (Vattimo, 1990).

It is interesting to add that in recent decades, culture has attempted to offer an answer which was unthinkable in the past, through medical technology, based on the power of the image and of appearance, inventing an artificial fate (Baudrillard, 1990). In this perspective, plastic surgery, prostheses and new reproductive techniques offer an illusion of immortality, either through eternal youth and beauty or through the possibility of producing children at formerly unimagined ages. This author considers that it is a kind of liberating mutation of the exigencies of time. The complexity of these proposals, which appeared at the turn of the century, resides in the offer of solutions and ways out of problems which were previously impossible to solve, while sometimes closing their potential inclusion in a symbolic network.

In the course of our discussions, we need to place the emphasis on the movements between rupture and creation involving crucial categories linked both to the psyche's capacity for symbolic re-composition and to the re-definition of ideals and identifications, in the face of logical and chronological temporal impacts. In clinical work, this means not only an opportunity to re-signify a genealogy but for each subject to create and invent his or her own metaphors. It also becomes a place to question the traditional feminine position.

CHAPTER FIVE

Love and power: the conditions of love in the Freudian discourse

This chapter centres on the different forms of discourse regarding love in relation to power and sexual difference, its point of departure being the Freudian discourse. This involves illuminating the psychic spaces in which power and love develop, referring them to fundamental splitting in psychic life. We particularly consider how these conditions variously affect the vicissitudes of love, sexual desire and passion in both sexes.

Concerning a condition of love

In "A special type of choice of object made by men", Freud (1910) aptly describes a condition of loving in men in which the choice of object is based on love for "easy" women ("love for a prostitute"). The characteristic of these women is that they are highly prized objects of love and at the same time replaceable, so that a long series is formed. This condition of love includes the existence of an injured third party. This particular type of object choice can be observed in a variety which ranges between individuals with certain isolated features of it and cases with the complete typology. This choice is rooted in the splitting of the tender from the sensual currents expressed in the dissociation between mother and prostitute, and refers to the vicissitudes of the Oedipus complex.

Freud considers that in normal love life, a woman's value is ruled by her sexual integrity, so that the feature of being easy depreciates her. Thus in Freudian terms there is a *value*—as a more or less rigid consensus of acceptance—which determines that what is normal in a woman's love life is her sexual integrity. This integrity implies a virtuous condition which defines a woman as "normal" and worthy of being loved. In this context these values implicitly differ from those which define the masculine position, in which a virtuous or virginal life would disqualify masculinity. This knowledge about love forms is—in terms of values—one of the strongest discourses on the difference between the feminine and the masculine positions. Thus the figure of the Don Juan is formed as the prototype of the man who desires all women but loves none. And thus the figure of the woman who gives priority to love over desire, especially in the form of being loved, is also formed. These configurations respond to imaginary constructions which, when they become universal, affect and condition each subject's singular position.

We need to remember that the values Freud refers to are part of a vigorous discourse whose collision with other present forms of discourse generates tensions with still unpredictable consequences for the conditions of accessing subjectivity in both sexes. This leads us to investigate the interwoven connections and oppositions between the *episteme* inherent in each period of time, the differential kinds of discourse on sexual difference, the constitution of the psychic apparatus and the drive activity. On this point we need to make it clear that it is impossible to think about the feminine position in terms of a universal category, but neither do we work with the idea of absolute singularity, which can only be conceptualized in clinical practice. We will position ourselves in an intermediate space where the universal is questioned, while accepting the existence of certain shared variables which permit us to advance on the subject of female subjectivity.

In "On the universal tendency to debasement in the sphere of love" (1912), Freud maintains that psychic impotence characterizes the love life of the cultured man. Its most universal content is an incestuous fixation which leads to a splitting of the affectionate and the sensual currents. Only in a minority do the two currents fuse, when respect for women is overcome and the representation of incest accepted. This is to say that men nearly always achieve full potency with a debased object.

But how would this affect women, considering that this splitting takes place either partially or totally in men? According to Freud, in our cultural world women are under the influence of an after-effect as a reaction to men's behaviour. This generates an unfavourable effect, whether they are approached without full potency or they are debased and depreciated. In this line of thinking, if women choose the respectable or accepted place, they have to restrict their sensuality; and if they choose sensuality, they will have to bear debasement.

This theory, according to which *women are subject to an after-effect as a reaction to men's behaviour*, shows us a paradoxical position for women. *Neither the virtuous condition nor full sensuality is possible*; there is no choice, which creates a *prescribed alternative of alienation*. Virtue signals the impossible, considering that sensuality is not an option because of the risk of debasement. Thus sensuality would pre-figure an eventual contingency: her fall as a "debased object". The latter position condenses two tendencies for the feminine position: on the one hand heavy narcissistic depreciation, and on the other hand the formation of a phantasy of prostitution (Aulagnier, 1967). Freud adds that this debasement of the sexual object does not occur in women, since the object is not previously overestimated. There is instead a prolonged thwarting of everything sexual and the withdrawal of sensuality into fantasy. This determines the union between prohibition and sensual activity. The *prohibited condition* is comparable to the debasement of sex life in the male. This condition is at the roots of the passionate relationship.

On the other hand, when Freud switches from the perspective of the choice of object to the viewpoint of the drive, he affirms that there is something in the sexual drive itself which is unfavourable to the achievement of full satisfaction. He adds that cultural dissatisfaction is a necessary consequence of certain characteristics which the sexual drive has acquired as a consequence of the pressure imposed by culture. He also goes on to say that frustration increases the psychic signification of the sexual drive.

These considerations lead us to underscore that the *intersection between the absence—by definition—of full drive satisfaction and the after-effect on women of men's behaviour, generated by the splitting of the men's tender and sensual currents, is at the root of many problems in connection with the feminine condition that we see in our consulting rooms* (frigidity, feelings of devaluation). Moreover, we believe that this intersection conditions a certain type of object choice in women, in which love and sexual desire are split off (with the predominance of love), although, as we have seen, for reasons that differ from men's.

Therefore, *within this logical frame* there is no possible resolution of the female position in regard to sensuality and sexual desire. Here, at the core of this splitting, love arises with special intensity. *Love as the preferential way out, in view of the non-resolution of the prescribed alternative of alienation: neither virtue nor sensuality.* In this context we can understand Freud's affirmation that castration anxiety in men is equivalent to women's anxiety facing the object-loss or, more precisely, the loss of the object's love itself.

Mother-child permeation and power

We know that this splitting of the tender and the sensual currents in men responds to an incestuous fixation. The maternal imago is preserved absolutely through the tender current, although it appears again as the degraded woman in the sensual current. If we include the power dimension as another category, that splitting would also be present in the "horror" of submission to the all-powerful pre-oedipal mother, the horror of being violently trapped by that power.

Medusa's head also refers to the mother's terrifying genitals, an allusion to the mother's "castration", which Freud (1940) considers as leading to castration anxiety in males. The "terror" of Medusa's head is associated with a vision based on a previous perspective and theoretical interpretation. No threat of castration is possible without previous signification, in the manner of infantile sexual theories; that is, a threat of loss of potency and of feminization. But is there not a recognition of the power attributed to the mother, whose "castration"—with all the semantic power it implies—would thus be necessary in order to keep this threat on the outside?

We think that this configuration is based on a primary splitting of a "feminine moment" for both sexes, when mother-child permeation signals an exclusive relation with the passive position predominant for either the son or the daughter.[1] A moment lacking words but full of feelings and perceptions, which is debilitating in the sense that it is subject to maternal power. At the same time, its rigid splitting—mainly in the male—permits the affirmation of a flawless masculinity, but preserving the "horror" forever fresh. This splitting is the expression of a vector of power relations on which, through the maternal discourse, positions are pegged for the imaginary construction of masculinity and femininity, through identifications and ideals.

In this primordial space, love is the privileged agent of transmission of the shared imaginary proposals that define desirable positions for men or women, which the parental unconscious attaches to the child's gender, materializing into ideal identifications. These discourse productions act on the girl's or boy's body and cause effects of truth to circulate, as well as empty psychic spaces and silences in regard to sexual difference.

***

The great maternal divinities of the Oriental peoples had the potential to engender and annihilate. Freud worked on these aspects in "The theme of the three caskets" (1913), in which he refers to the goddesses of life, fertility and death. Maternal power generates ambivalence and also acquires formalization in myths or in individual fantasy. However, we point out that this refers to a significant contradiction, since on the one hand maternal power incarnates the great phenomena of life and death, fate and fertility, while on the other this power contrasts with frequent problems in relation to the drop in self-esteem and devaluation that we detect in clinical practice with women.

This is one of the most complex knots in the theory. Expressed in its full development, it could trace one of the itineraries of sexual desire in Freud's writings and his questions about women. In the Freudian affirmation that the three types of relationships of men with women are those with the mother, with the beloved—in the mother's image—and with the Mother Earth, we clearly see that the mother is the guiding thread in these relationships. The forever unresolved problem is the temptation and search for the mother, seat of power and of an original incestuous *jouissance*, which the "imperative" of masculinity forces to split radically. This radicality thwarts love life in the male, so he can only express himself in a split-off way between sexual desire and love. We must point out that this is supported by

the imaginary figure of a "drive mother", "ensnaring and devouring", with no potential of her own to create a symbolic space.[2]

It is necessary to underscore that this splitting is radical, in direct
proportion to the threat of being reduced to passivity. Further, we
consider that it articulates with the splitting of the tender and sensual
currents in men, which saves them (in their phantasy) from remaining submissive to the all-powerful mother. The separation of
love from sexual desire permits them to avoid the route to love that
would imply a potential threat of substituting the wife for the mother
(Aulagnier, 1967). Nonetheless, we emphasize that this protection
costs them some impoverishment in regard to the development of
their love life. On the other hand, this primordial splitting lateralizes
and fades the feminine figure, which is then subsumed into the
mother's. This means that *there is no remaining psychic space for a female
subject beyond the maternal.* We need to highlight that this holds true
for both sexes.

This results in another *after-effect* on women, an effect which is at
the root of their difficulties in constructing subjectivity, since only
maternity could create effects of symbolization. In this context, we
return to the problem of the absence of symbolization of the feminine.
Irigaray (1992) notes that the Romance languages have no grammar
for women, in the sense that the universal belongs to men. The
linguistic order excludes the female gender, so that the feminine is
simply a non-masculine. She considers that sexual difference informs
the language and is in turn informed by it. In this sense, we believe
that a field of lines of force is created between what can and what
cannot be represented, where specific configurations of power
develop, determining the conditions of love and sexual desire for
both sexes.

"Everything in the sphere of this first attachment to the mother
seemed to me so difficult to grasp in analysis—so grey with age and
shadowy and almost impossible to revivify—that it was as if it had
succumbed to an especially inexorable repression," as Freud (1931)
wrote. Is there some echo of the primarily maternal, wordless, the
most familiar and ancient, which becomes foreign and uncanny? This
is why he appeals to the help of the transference with female analysts
when the pre-oedipal phase is revealed to him.

Finally, the Freudian itinerary leads him to conclude that a
marriage is not ensured until the wife has been able to make her

husband her son as well as to act towards him like a mother. In the frame of this logic, the fate of femininity is maternity: women are subsumed into the mother as a *princeps* form of subjectivity. In this context we can interpret his affirmation: "One gets an impression that a man's love and a woman's are a phase apart psychologically" (Freud, 1933 [1932]). This closes a logical, theoretical and interpretive circle which determines, in the Freudian opus, the strict and powerful conditions legislating love and object choice for both sexes. These conditions relate to the way in which both sexes position themselves in relation to incompleteness and to the effects of power which are configured between them. In these gaps, in these psychic spaces generated by primordial splitting in relation to the primary object; in these lines of force that have developed between what can and what cannot be represented, between subject and object, the universal and the contingent, the active and the passive, love develops, as we shall see, marked by relations of power-domination that are an intrinsic component of the relations between men and women.

Taboo and power

We know that Freud (1918) attributes the primitive peoples' taboo of virginity basically to the attempt to avoid the female's hostile reaction to the male who deflowers her. This is why, in these societies, virgins are not deflowered by their husbands. But Freud goes a bit further and concludes that women are entirely taboo for men. They are foreign and hostile: different, mysterious, and thus hostile. This is why men fear being weakened or feminized, a situation still vigorous in contemporary culture. It is important to point out that since women are presented as being different to the norm, the masculine, they carry a mystery, and a *power* is attributed to them. The taboo is set up in the face of danger: only something powerful can be dangerous. But the absolute power belongs to the omnipotent pre-oedipal mother. Not so much to the wife, since the fear of feminization is a cultural paradigm of the loss of power-potency. For men, to be feminized is a symbol of weakness and passivity.

Freud goes on to say that women's hostility generates servitude: paradoxically, they do not rid themselves of their husband unless they do not take revenge. Frigidity is also a consequence of these hostile motions. He advances still further, highlighting that

monogamy applies to women and that sexual servitude is indispensable for damming up the polygamous impulses, since it ensures
the possession of women. This opens a field of reflection on the
exercise of power, without excluding the position of servitude. The
consequence is women's ambivalence, which conditions a profuse
fantasy life and the search for a "forbidden passion". This is the
source of the ways in which the feminine position is marked in
relation to love, falling in love, passion and seduction.

We also recall that Lévi-Strauss (1949) posited that the basis of
social organization and the passage to culture is the positioning
of women as objects of exchange. We note also that Freud (1923)
places the feminine, the passive and the object in the same series.
Lacan (1972–73) underscores that women, as *object a*, are cause and
object of sexual desire. This position as object of sexual desire, as
object a, as well as the mythical category of taboo, generates certain
conditions of love in and towards women, which are inherent in this
logic. The result is the conjunction of a series of variables among
which relations of power develop:

1. The splitting of the tender from the sensual current in men
    and its after-effect in women places the latter in a paradoxical
    position with no possible resolution in regard to the relation
    between the sensual and the tender. Power is exercised in
    relations both of love and desire.
2. The splitting of the primary object, an operation aimed at
    annulling its power, is more radical in the male because of
    the threat to his masculinity, but always exposes him to the
    risk that this object may return in the figure of his beloved.
3. The condition of the female as being taboo in the sense
    of something foreign and threatening, and as such a seat of
    power, with its counterpart, the woman's hostility and sexual
    servitude. These variables signal the conditions in which love
    can become servitude; sexual desire can go through infinite
    substitutions; seduction can serve to reassure being; or
    prohibition become an unavoidable condition of sensuality.
    This depends on the position taken by each individual.

In this sense, the Freudian theoretical frame expresses a dimension
of knowledge and discourse on sexual difference, with heavy support

from a shared phantasy which associates sexual desire with the masculine position and love with the feminine position.

Power and conditions of love

The mother-child bond, as well as the relationship between a man and a woman or any other human relationship, consists of power relations, productive spaces, transmission belts. This is power in the sense Foucault gives it (1979, 1984): relations of forces between two or more points which can be mobile and changing, with a configuration of their own and a relative autonomy, and not necessarily a reflection of any greater power. Power relations are inherent in any relationship and, in the words of Deleuze (1986), the categories of power are: induce, incite, shape, deviate, facilitate or obstruct, expand or limit. In this perspective, any relation of love is also one of power. It may even be exercised in the line of dominator *versus* dominated. But power is not the same as domination, since relations of domination convert the other into an object and therefore block the potential to structure an intersubjective relation. When power becomes fixed as domination, a dimension of violence is established in a present tense of pure repetition. The field of domination is static and rigid, while power is mobile and temporal. Whether the power relation becomes a power/domination relation depends on the line in which it develops: repetition and fate *versus* difference and temporality. These relations of power-domination may or may not coincide with each subject's phantasies of domination and submission.

In Freudian theory, the different conditions for the choice of the love object in the male or the female signal a certain stability or fixedness in the development of relations of power-domination. Since sexual desire is mobile and functions through displacement and substitution, it lends itself to affirming masculinity and exerting a domination which is supported by its non-dependence on the object, since the latter may be replaced.

On the other hand and in this frame, love functions for the female as a condition of sexual desire, and being loved represents the narcissistic recognition that may allow her to develop her desire, a development that always involves a risk of narcissistic devaluation. This condition is at the base of women's excessive dependence on love and of the amorous servitude described by Freud. We must add that this dependence on love may also be a different way of exercising power-domination. The power of love resides in showing the other that he or she is essential and indispensable for existence itself, for the integrity of being, so that it becomes a relation of domination.

We also need to clarify the interrelations and differences between love, falling in love and passion. In this context, falling in love, seen as a narcissistic exacerbation and extreme idealization, has different functions in both sexes. According to Freudian contributions, in men it is at the service of sexual desire, and can follow its own itinerary or become fixed on an impossible woman. For women it may provide access to the order of passion and through it to a journey on the road of sexual desire, or otherwise avoid it through platonic love.

Both love and falling in love have narcissistic roots. But love involves recognition of the object as an other, while falling in love implies that the object is ignored in favour of narcissistic gratification. In this perspective, therefore, love is neither a limitless fusion with the object nor a simple re-edition of the primary relation with the mother; nor is it only a present without past or future, inherent in a passionate-drive dimension. However, the latter dimension arises when there is threat of a break in the Unity, generating a passionate wish to return to the mother's body. This means that even though love includes conditions of a passionate nature, it also produces a *plus*: it produces difference as well. Love implies the recognition of limits, of finitude, of the Other, not only as an object but as a subject possessing a specific history, a singular body and a particular itinerary of sexual desire. Love is therefore a love of finitudes, one's own and others', in the words of Trías (1983).

In this way, the lethal condition of passion, in the thanatic dimension, can be re-launched through love towards recognition of finitude and of difference itself. It also means that in love a passionate drive condition is preserved, with a corporeal anchorage, in a complex and unstable configuration. In consequence, we are led to salvage a facet of passion which is necessary for amorous life, for sublimation and for creativity, and is indispensable in this intermediate space. This interpretation leads us to see love as a hinge operating in a border zone of intersections. This is why we take up the discourse of Plato, in which Diotima situates love as something intermediate between the beautiful and the ugly, between good and evil, the divine and the mortal; it is neither rich nor poor, mortal nor immortal: it is *Daimon*. In the same way we can think of it as an operator between the imaginary and the symbolic, as an intermediary between repetition and difference, between fate and choice, between atemporal and historical dimensions.

***

Thus we return to our point of departure: the Freudian discourse on love and the splitting of love and sexual desire, different in men and in women. In these contributions we underscore a primordial splitting in relation to the primary object, whose radicality marks a split-off condition of love in men, which generates an after-effect in women. *This is then submitted to the rigorous laws of a paradoxical logic— neither virtue nor sensuality—which finds no resolution within this discourse.*

In the frame of this splitting, we emphasize the existence of power-domination relations, which configure psychic spaces where love develops. This splitting is produced in a relational inter-subjective context, inserted in a logical construction which creates a fixedness that appears imaginarily to be immovable. As we have proposed, this fixedness tends to establish static relations of domination, leaving little space for the mobility and temporality inherent in relations of power.

We differentiate love from falling in love, both having narcissistic roots. But in love the object is recognized as Other, with its singularity and its history. All love is rooted in passion; however, love surpasses the blind Fate of repetition: it adds a *plus* which signals difference itself.

Notes

1. Jones (1927), Winnicott (1966), Greenson (1968) and other authors have pointed out this question from different perspectives.
2. Cf. Chapter Seven for other theoretical proposals on maternity.

CHAPTER SIX

Itineraries of love life

Discourse and ideals

Figures of love run through human history: filial love, maternal love, love between a man and a woman, homosexual love, the love of God. We find great love stories in literature and in myths: Romeo and Juliet, Don Juan, the Olympian loves between gods and mortals, the jealous love of Othello, interspersed with everyday love stories. We also know that love is part of the origins of psychoanalysis, and bring to mind the unhappy loves of Elizabeth von R., Dora, the young homosexual and Schreber. And fundamentally, that Freud introduces a new twist when he considers love as an instrument in the process of the cure and includes it in the analytic experience.

This leads us to what we could call the two facets of love: love as repetition and love as a project, and in this context we will try to elucidate the way in which the ideals interact with these two currents of the amorous experience. On the basis of this proposal, I examine two lines of development: courtly love and mother-child love. In both, I point out the concomitant power relations and their connections with the ideals involved.

Courtly love

We have to consider that the Freudian contributions are based on the codes of courtly love. However, although it is true that Freud takes this model, we also note that he breaks these codes when he introduces the concept of the unconscious in his theoretical discussions.

In modern times, medieval courtly love—one of the types of love in the amorous exchange between men and women—was established as an ideal in the couple. It was supported by the idealization of the woman—the Lady—and the troubadours were its model. Kristeva (1992) points out that the troubadours met together in fraternal-type groups with ties of homosexual love. Thus the idealization of the Lady was organized as a cover-up. The idealization of the feminine functions as a brake for anxiety: basically anxiety in relation to sexual difference. Courtly love was also based on power relations, which it expressed. On the one hand, it could have been a tactic of the subject to attract the object and exercise his power, since the Lady was not considered a person but an object: the seat of wealth and power, or possessing an inaccessible virginity that had to be conquered. On the other hand, paradoxically, this idealization was an attempt to neutralize the power attributed to the Lady (Kristeva, 1992).

The hidden face of the idealized woman is the fallen woman. This interplay of opposites is based on the repudiation, hate or implicit ignorance of the Other. The detractors of courtly love expressed these ideas. In praise of polygamy, Schopenhauer (1966) considered it necessary to remove the Lady from her pedestal. In his opinion, the Lady was a monster of European civilization with her ridiculous pretensions of respect and honour. And, he added, she must be reduced to her true role: of subordination.

These debates express the splitting between the idealized woman and the fallen woman. We have to consider that the Lady's power was limited in reality because she was a woman; not so the residue of the ancient power of the mother, which lies at the root of this splitting.[1] Just as we highlighted in the previous chapter, Freud (1910, 1912) emphasizes the dissociation we commonly find in the cultured man between the idealized mother and the prostitute. This splitting is heavily supported by the need to avoid the incestuous attraction of the primary object, an imperative of masculinity in the male. This leads to a splitting between sexual desire and love in the male, with desire predominant. The background of this splitting is, as mentioned earlier, the remnant of an old debt to the mother.

From this the following problem results: in a masculine position, men should uphold this splitting, which generates a paradoxical alternative for women. The mother position has maximum value, but is opposed to sensuality, while the position which develops sensuality involves narcissistic depreciation. *Both positions involve loss or devaluation, leaving no choice, this being an unavoidable reference to the specific alienations of the female position inherent in this logic.* These Freudian contributions are related to knowledge and discourse on love in which women are placed in a feminine position organized around the demand of love, while men are psychically organized around successive substitutions of sexual desire, which pertain to ideal figurations of the heterosexual relationship.

We therefore see the coexistence of two models of love in the Freudian opus. On the one hand is love as it was viewed in Antiquity, as an aspiration in which the least perfect tends to the most perfect. That is, the love aimed from the lover's imperfection towards the perfection of the beloved: the Lady of courtly love, the wife-mother as an ideal. On the other hand is love in the Christian sense, as *caritas*, the tendency of the most perfect or the superior to descend to the inferior and imperfect, for example to love the fallen woman.

Mother-child love: clinical reference

For the discussion of this point, I will refer briefly to the situation of a forty-six year old woman, a divorcee with a particular relationship of amorous dependence with her mother, in a passionate current of fascination. The salient feature of this relationship was its tint of affective homogeneity, with disavowal of unpleasurable affects. On the contrary, there was a special feeling of satisfaction and admiration for the mother, with only occasional and tepid expressions of aggressiveness.

This woman had come to see me for symptoms of anxiety and diffuse fears, associated with frequent choking and heartburn. She had married when she was twenty-one and had a daughter, only to separate soon afterwards and return to live with her parents. She worked, while her mother brought up her daughter. The father was a secondary character in this constellation. We can mention some significant facts:

1. The death of a sister two years older, a place she was meant to fill as a substitute of her dead sister.

2. Her special fascination for her mother's eyes. She said, "When she looks at me, it is something special, she's fascinating, she attracts everybody." She repeated these phrases in an infantile tone of voice; it was a little girl's voice. This was the way she conveyed her state of defencelessness facing the mother's gaze and word, immersed in a hypnotic fascination which had a passionate quality.

3. Her position was an accepted, comfortable position, and the idealized object was part of herself. No other amorous relationship, not even with her current partner, with whom she didn't live; not even with her daughter, could equal the intensity of her relationship with her mother.

4. Her identification with the mother in her rejection of men was the continuation of a matriarchal line which ran from her grandmother: the saga prescribed that in her family the women had no need of men except to procreate. This expressed the power of the maternal lineage.

5. This love was also placed at the service of an interminable psychic processing by the mother, referred to a traumatic mourning in relation to her dead daughter. In this context, the patient was situated as the mother's fetish daughter, in an endogamous circuit where giving the mother a child appeared to be a necessary compensation. Her fidelity ensured the mother's psychic stability.

This brief description emphasizes the currents of power-domination in relations of passionate, amorous dependency, which are at the root of narcissistic relationships. In this case it was an attempt to psychically process the un-worked-through mourning, sometimes coming from former generations.

Love is a force inherent in any relationship, which seeks and conveys significations. We see that it is a necessary and unavoidable component of primary relations which cannot be dissociated from the use of power; however, because of the asymmetry which characterizes these relations, it can easily slip into the category of domination and/or violence.

The primary object is a source of frequently conflicting sexual desires and of imaginary but powerful identifying enunciates which come into play in the intersubjective field, where they can generate psychic inscriptions configuring mandates of fate. In this context, the concept of thirdness breaks up the One of the dual, fusional relationship and generates a potential to develop other itineraries.

An open system

On the basis of the above discussion, I propose to differentiate idealization as narcissistic closure from the preservation of ideals which are indispensable in the amorous experience as a type of social tie. Because the roots of love lie deep in the need for an ideal inherent in being human, we inevitably traverse the field of the ideals in the register of love. The trajectories of love are based on narcissism of the origins which encompasses self-love and love of the ideals to which we aspire. Freud (1914) distinguished the anaclitic choice of the object of love from the narcissistic choice. This differentiation is actually coexistence. Both are supported by original narcissism and, in a certain sense, ensure the subject's narcissism.

We see that in the amorous experience, the ego expands and goes beyond its limits, although we recall something Freud showed us: it is the ego that loves. In this sense, Kristeva (1983) points out that love is the time and space in which the ego concedes itself the right to be extraordinary. But considering love in a narcissistic, imaginary order is simply an opening approach to this issue. Therefore, if we are to advance further in this investigation, we need to consider that the amorous experience is not unidimensional, and that more than one level is involved in the conceptualizations of love.

We need to underscore that even though the amorous experience tends and aspires to the One or to totality, it finds that aspiration impossible to attain. The imaginary facet of the experience of love makes it a place of mistakes and deceits, but going beyond or crossing the frontiers of narcissism also makes it a place of confirmations, of contact with limits, separation and death. This crossing assumes recognition not only of the object but, beyond the object, of the Other. This refers not to the imaginary other or the fellow human, but to the Other as heterogeneous to oneself, which cannot be reduced to the subject.

Therefore, this means *thinking of the amorous experience as a system in connection with the Other: that is, configured as an open system*, a conception which differs from fusion love. This conception, based on human exchange, depends on the movements of aperture and unbalance that constitute stable organizations (Morin, 1990). The aperture of an open system is neither indifferent nor indiscriminate: this type of system is governed by its own specific laws. Further, this proposal also implies considering not only the relation with a heterogeneous Other, but also the heterogeneous elements inherent in each system (Kristeva, 1986).

In this context, we see that the idealization in the experience of falling in love and of passion-love can simulate an open system, even though it is actually narcissistic closure. This means that although love always circulates on the edges of passion, the latter adds a component of asymmetry and absence of reciprocity, as has already been stated by Aulagnier (1967). Passion implies domination of the object and addiction to it, in a dimension which can be lethal when the object becomes an object of necessity, as we observe in the clinical reference described above.

This leads us to transference love. Freud maintained that the capacity to love in life can be recovered through transference love. We know that transference love is no more than love, and we also know that love sustains listening. This makes it possible to develop an order of significations, de-centring the fixedness to pre-determined referents. Transference love allows us to expand frontiers as well as place limits regarding the construction of subjectivity. This is possible on condition that transference love is not satisfied, thus displacing it from the order of necessity. It also implies *considering the transference relation as an open system*, which includes the Other and allows for a complex symbolic organization. To be precise, considering the psyche as an *open system* can allow its renewal, through phenomena of order and disorder, in the sense described by Balandier (1990). This differs from deadly repetition. If it fails to occur in this way, the analyst, rather than a beloved other, becomes a factor of domination and submission, a perverse application of his or her power. Instead of providing a motor for the cure, the analyst becomes an instrument of repetition and death drive.

This makes the difference between love as a pure present, installed on the repetition compulsion, and the potential of love as *poiesis*, a production which generates a difference. *When love is production, the subject/object relation undergoes a change of place: the object of love becomes a subject*. It is no longer the necessary and absolute narcissistic

complement of the subject, but expresses the passage towards a
heterogeneous Other. This means passing from the insistence of a
pure present to the possibility of a prospective temporal dimension.[2]
It also signals the difference between the ideal ego and the ego ideal.
It makes the difference between the idealization of the beloved
object and the symbolic ideals that connect with a heterogeneous
Other. It is, as we noted elsewhere (1998), the symbolic mark that
produces difference as a category on the edges of the ideals.

We see that to speak of love implies speaking of passion, falling
in love, narcissism, object relation, the Other, and its relations to
sexual desire, pleasure, hate and indifference. This involves speaking
of polarities and binary thought: love/hate, love/indifference,
love/falling in love, love/passion. However, these dualities are not
symmetrical. Freud (1915) already observed that the origin of hate
differs from the origin of love. The pure pleasure ego recognizes
everything pleasurable as ego and everything unpleasurable as non-
ego or as object. Thus hate and indifference are associated with the
object as the first type of relationship with it: a source of unpleasure.

Love is therefore symmetrical neither with hate nor with
indifference. That is to say even though love comes into the binary
relations inherent in the dualism of language, these dichotomies
are broken precisely by their asymmetry, since their origins are
different. Consequently, although these polarities are presented as
having a binary relation, they surpass the binary thought of radical
oppositions because of their asymmetry, and thus enter the field of
complexity.

***

Finally, we find that the current crisis in amorous relations is
weakening social ties. However, at the same time, we observe that
the amorous ideals, be they Western or universal prototypes, are
preserved today as a wish. This leads us to propose the need to go
through and beyond these amorous ideals. We consider that there is
an inevitable passage through the two facets of the amorous ideals:
on the one hand the tendency to the One with its idealized and
absolute components, and on the other a contact with incompleteness,
finitude and difference.

The latter configuration implies, as we have said, a passage from the object to the Other and from the idealized other to the Other that is heterogeneous to the subject. This makes the difference between fusion and illusion on the one hand, and reciprocity and creative enhancement on the other. It implies the distinction between an open and a closed system; between love as an intermediary between the ego and the Other and love as a block to the ego-Other relation, with annulment of the Other in favour of an absolutism of the ego.

The amorous experience is not unidimensional: there is no single perspective in the conceptualizations on love. Therefore, our proposal is to think that in the amorous experience, there is an aspiration to totality, an ideal of unification, which reaches its height in falling in love and in passion. However, it is also impossible to access that totality. This is another facet of love in which the ideals are limited, and this impossible unification evidences incompleteness and finitude. Entering and leaving ideals, idealizing and de-idealizing, is one of the paths on the road of love. It makes the difference between love as pure present, as repetition, and love as a project, in production.

Notes

1. Cf. Chapter Five.
2. As Deleuze (1972) pointed out in regard to the works of Proust, what is sought in love is to discover the possible worlds the other carries and, at the same time, the subject's own.

CHAPTER SEVEN

Maternity and female sexuality in the light of the new reproductive techniques

Updating a debate

Psychoanalysts have been confronted in their clinical practice with innumerable conflicts, anxieties and questions about the relation between women and maternity. The analyst's theoretical conceptions can oscillate from understanding it as a fundamentally biological experience, deeply rooted in instinct, to considering it a category constructed only by culture; from emphasizing the drive component to placing it in the frame of object relations; they may "sexualize" the maternal figure or not; they may consider female sexuality isomorphic with maternity or not. The intercrossing between the theoretical perspective the psychoanalyst takes, his or her institutional filiations and transferences, and the way personal fantasies are resolved will be at the root of his or her interpretations, constructions and interventions concerning these problems, and this will have consequences in the analytic process.

Since the origins of culture, there has been no doubt about what a mother is. Narratives about the certainty of maternity always contrasted with the doubts and lack of evidence about paternity. Today, genetic studies provide certainties for paternity too, if we wish to accept this point of view as a parameter. However, the generation and development of new reproductive techniques challenges these certainties. Genetic, biological and nurturing maternity are aspects which do not necessarily coincide. This forces us to re-formulate questions about the concepts of maternity and paternity. To this we add the possibility of postponing the moment of maternity or even some women's decision not to be mothers. Old arguments acquire new vigour and new questions are imposed.

In the new century, vertiginous development of medical technology presents new problems and ethical dilemmas which are difficult to resolve. Assisted fertilization (with a couple's own or another couple's gametes), the rental of a uterus, sperm banks, frozen embryos, cloning, experiments in genetic engineering: these are some of the novel solutions and increasingly sophisticated proposals which are expanding geometrically. Their characteristics and consequences make it hard to process and inscribe them psychically.

The case of Ana is a small example. She is a woman aged 39, who feels anguished because she is reaching the reproductive age limit and is afraid she won't be able to have children. She consults a gynaecologist, who offers to freeze her ovules so that she can use them in the future. This is a minimum proposal in comparison to the very complex possibilities we have mentioned. However, Ana cannot process this psychically, although it would be a practical solution for the problem she went to see the gynaecologist about. In the course of analysis, quite active mourning processes are revealed, including two abortions and the death of a grandmother who had great emotional importance in her childhood. Her relationship with her own mother, whose word was always law, was extremely dependent. Ana complained of her failures with successive partners, although her choices inevitably implied that she was going to be rejected. Thus, in the course of her analysis, the reason for consulting the gynaecologist was de-centred and unexpected phantasmatic paths were generated. It is obvious that in this case the physician's proposal falls within the laws of supply and demand, and aims at considering maternity as a necessity—supported by a biological order—which must be met, with no consideration for Ana's psychic constellation. Medical knowledge fails to coincide with Ana's unconscious truth.

The undeniable contributions of the new reproductive techniques do not exclude consideration of the risks of manipulation and emphasis on reproduction as a biological mandate. This fact leaves aside the concept of maternity as desire and choice: that is, as a loving development in a constellation which broadly transcends the natural order. In addition, the growing possibility of being able to gestate a child to term outside the mother's body raises unprecedented questions concerning the material, corporeal support of maternity. The new reproductive techniques also create another kind of problem with regard to the genealogical fractures, broken or altered filiations that could occur. What does it mean to be a mother when a grandmother gestates her daughter's child in her womb? And what if this child were also the product of another woman's ovule? The limit between the possible and the impossible becomes blurred, and some proposals even border on the uncanny. What is the impact of the temporal dimension on the psyche when a twin is born many years after his brother? Or when a child is conceived with his dead father's frozen semen?

Changes in the nuclear family, the rise of narcissism in social discourse and sexual non-differentiation open the panorama to other questions. Is it enough to re-affirm that a mother is the one who desires, brings up, takes care of and loves her child? Is it the same if these conditions are met by one of the partners of a female homosexual couple, who could gestate a child with the aid of a sperm bank? Or by a couple of male homosexuals who rent a uterus for the same purpose? It is also undeniable that there are many other questions concerning paternity and its consequences for the child, but all of them are beyond the scope of this text. The main line of this proposal is to analyse the theoretical categories that support conceptions regarding maternity and female sexuality, with the intention of updating a debate inevitably activated by the new reproductive techniques. In this context, my intention is to salvage the decisive part that the desire for a child plays in its necessary relation with the techniques proposed.

Idealized and de-sexualized maternity

We can say that maternity is a category infrequently questioned by religions, philosophy and mythology. The figure of the idealized mother has had maximum cultural impregnation since the origins of culture. This figure is part of the sacred, the unquestionable, something that cannot be explained by reasoning. It is supported by a very powerful base: the mystery of the creation of life.

Maternity considered as a mandate of Nature supports the idea of an unavoidable female fate. This idea is the central "argument" of its idealization. Hence the need to differentiate reproduction from symbolic maternity, considering that the former belongs to the order of the natural and the latter implies a human experience where other planes are knit together: love, sexual desire, creativity. This differentiation also involves integration: there is a corporeal support, always erogenous and signified, on which the maternal experience is produced. The other argument supporting this idealized condition is the virgin mother, a heavily impregnating construction in Christianity. The condensation of maternity/virginity, under the rhetorical figure known as an *oxymoron*, tends to de-sexualize maternity and femininity. These aspects come together in conceiving of maternity as an ideal category, as an idealization of an original narcissistic state that represents a "paradise lost" which the child imaginarily experienced and the adult cannot stop constructing (Kristeva, 1983).

In men, the idealized mother and the de-sexualized woman operates as an imaginary antidote for castration anxiety. For women, this idealization shows a road that frames them in a given symbolic order. Having a child will thus represent the potential to reach a category of universality. However, the idealization of the maternal is a source of dissatisfaction for some women, since other aspects of the feminine are ignored. A type of discontent in today's culture is the swing between joy over a nourishing and loving maternity and dissatisfaction with the renunciation of autonomous sexuality, or sublimations and other creative projects. We must also point out that the idealization of maternity can be organized as a masquerade, in which case it would conceal the emphasis on the purely reproductive, instinctive and natural aspects of the maternal experience.

The phenomenon of idealization of maternity in women has great theoretical and clinical consequences. The mother, to the extent that she enters into the category of the sacred, the idolized, will be considered the person mainly responsible for her child's fate. To this we could add that the idealization of the maternal condition implies the temptation to retain the child in order to restore an imaginary totality. This idealization also tends to suppress the aggressive components and the ambivalence in the mother-child relationship. The tensions with the ideal, inherent in the maternal function, are stretched to the limit with idealization. A field develops in which the inevitable failure concerning expectations of absolute agreement between the mother and the child may impregnate the maternal experience with feelings of inadequacy.

The two faces of woman

The split between maternity and sexuality is a mark of the dilemmas that affect women's psychosexual development. The woman/mother equivalence appears as an alibi in the face of this dilemma, expressing the tendency to give priority to female subjectivity through maternity, in an attempt to regulate the bonds between women and men just as an established order has determined.

In "The Theme of the Three Caskets", Freud (1913) maintains that men find the figure of the mother under three forms in the course of their life: "the mother herself; the beloved one who is chosen after her pattern, and lastly the Mother Earth who receives him once more". In this way, Freud proposes that there is a pregnant presence of the mother in the man's love life, with the consequent attraction and rejection of incest which is at the base of the idealization of the maternal figure and which prevents him overcoming completely the splitting mentioned above.

***

In Rita's case, the desire for a child arose, though ambivalently, after she had already passed the biological age limit. Ambivalence was always central in her relationship with her mother. Her father, weak and impotent, was a marginal figure in her life. In the course of her analysis and through the transference, tremendous hostility towards her mother began to come into focus, a mother she felt was the sole depository of a dangerous sexuality and an absolute maternity which included a mandate forbidding her to be a mother in her turn.

For Rita, there was a condensation between the all-powerful, idealized mother, who was hated because of her power, and the sexual mother equated with a prostitute. The mother/woman conjunction, imaginarily embodied by the figure of her own mother, was one of the roots of her finding it impossible to establish a couple relationship, at the same time eternalizing her as a daughter subjected to an absolute maternal law. In her phantasm, the idealized mother with thanatic characteristics carried a mandate of Fate which prevented Rita from becoming a mother; but her mother also appeared as the sole possessor of an indiscriminate and threatening sexuality. Her difficulty in undoing these equivalences in their phantasmatic concatenation was part of her analytic process. During her analysis she created symbolic equivalences of maternity. The equation sexuality + desire = prostitution, which made it impossible for her to establish a sexuality free of the laws and mandates coming from her own mother, was undone.

The question concerning the relation between maternity and female sexuality has not been fully explored. As a symbolic construction, maternity has always been equated with femininity in religious texts, myths, philosophy and medical texts. Thus femininity is presented as being subsumed by maternity in an isomorphism which is a mark of civilization. Maternity as an entity has been considered a universal representation contrasted with the absence of symbolization that some theoretical lines propose for the feminine condition. In this way the woman/mother equation obscures the idea of a feminine sexuality which would be autonomous in relation to maternity.

The exclusion of sexuality is a key element in idealized conceptions of maternity. This implies on the one hand exclusion of the erotic and libidinal conditions that ground the experience of maternity, and on the other hand the exclusion of sexuality and desire outside the domain of maternity. The consequences are great: on the one hand the tendency to ignore any aspect of the female condition that transcends maternity, and on the other hand the neglect of theory and practice to develop the multiple implications of maternity itself.

Psychoanalytic conceptions

We may recall that Freud (1925, 1931) defines three paths for the psychosexual development of the girl: inhibition or frigidity, the masculinity complex and maternity. The three are guided by penis envy, a consequence of the castration complex in the little girl. For Freud, the desire for a child is one of the ways that penis envy is resolved: when the girl turns from the mother to the father she places herself in the position of the positive Oedipus complex, and through the symbolic equation penis = child begins to wish for a baby from her father, and later on from another man. In these developments, maternity is a phallic aim, even though Freud considers it the great aim of female sexual desire. Moreover, none of these three orientations include a path for female sexuality which would be independent of maternity, frigidity or the masculinity complex. In this context, hysteria and femininity would be indissoluble.

Nevertheless, this logic contributes a conception of maternity responding to the driving force of desire that also develops in the Freudian conceptions of the mother as the initial seducer. Thus a notion of sexually grounded maternity implies the inauguration and marking of erogenous zones by the mother on the ground of the child's own drives. The conception of maternity as a phallic category is supported by a fetishistic argument: that the child is the mother's phallus. This has led some authors (Granoff & Perrier, 1979) to define a perversion inherent in the female condition, by extending the concept of perversion to one of the ways the maternal-filial relationship can develop.

Freud (1933) opens another road, not developed as fully, and finally subsumed by the former, concerning the girl's identification with her mother. This identification is supported by the passage from the passive to the active, and is manifested in playing with dolls. This conception develops an imaginary space concerning the maternal position; however, it also has a symbolic content provided by the mother in the intersubjective relationship with its codes, legislation and configurations.

Object relations theories have accentuated aspects relating to holding and caregiving, developing a concept of the mother/child relationship sustained by the relational aspect and the vicissitudes of object relations. Some aspects have departed from the instinctual conception, though running the risk of de-sexualizing the mother/child relationship.

Winnicott (1959) develops the concept of a transitional space which develops in the mother-child dyad as a playing space for creativity. He offers a different dimension to that of the "entrapping and devouring mother", since his proposal grounds the possibilities of separation, creation and autonomy.

Another question in debate is the existence of a maternal instinct in women. Chodorow (1978) considers that the upbringing of children inevitably tied to women is not a fact of nature. On the contrary, this author thinks that it results from the sexual division of labour, and from the separation of public and private domains. This creates the conditions for transmission in girls, through the relational aspect of upbringing, of dispositions and identifications for the experience of maternity.

I would point out that some schemes tend to consider maternity from the child's perspective: in the child's mind, the mother is all-powerful and absolute. These elements uphold the conception of a primary *jouissance* in the order of incest. It can lead to idealization of the maternal figure, an idealization which proceeds to subsume female sexuality within maternity. When these two categories are viewed as equivalent, the threat of incest is activated. *It is indispensable to emphasize that the child's perspective, with its theories and fantasies, as well as the constructions generated by the adult about him or her as a child, do not necessarily coincide, nor are they superimposed on the mother's perspective.*

The intersubjective dimension

From Freud (1914) onward, the narcissistic component operating in maternity has been highlighted. This alludes to the wish for completeness in the mother-child dyad, which only the father's intervention could break. "His Majesty the Baby" refers to infantile narcissism, to the mythical origins of "Paradise lost".

However, the configuration of the mother-child dyad on a narcissistic axis also has a structuring function. It implies the establishment of imaginary identifications and the development of a mirror dimension, where the mother's gaze is one of the organizing poles. But the child too, as a narcissistic extension, can embody unfulfilled ideals or be the object of a thanatic mandate, a condition that tends to perpetuate the dyadic organization. Nevertheless, if maternity were an exclusively narcissistic condition, no cut-off or separation would be possible, and the dyad would be eternal and indestructible.

It is important to note that maternal love, in spite of its narcissistic roots, is not univocal: we must differentiate narcissistic love, which fails to recognize the child as an object of desire, from object-love, which upholds the child's recognition and differentiation and which is at the foundation of his or her acceptance as an Other. The former is at the base of the repetition compulsion, as a thanatic mandate for a child who is an undifferentiated extension of the mother; the latter recognizes the difference, the limits and the separation.

With the recognition of the mother as the initial seducer, Freud contributes an erotic dimension linked to the marking of erogenous zones. Green (1997), for his part, aims to recover the heuristic value of maternal eroticism towards the child.

We consider that the aspects discussed above can be shaped into a broader organization if we consider the intersubjective dimension of the mother-child relationship. This includes the presence of a narcissistic frame, of sensuality (Alizade, 1992), caregiving, tenderness, love and attachment (Bowlby, 1969), together with the development of sexual desire and eroticism, in a complex interweave of conjunctions and disjunctions from subject to subject. The intersubjective configuration, though asymmetric, enables us to think in relational and more comprehensive terms to include all the variables involved.

It is important to show that even when the mother is everything for the child, since this is the expression of the earliest emotional tie with another person, before or co-existing with the object-cathexes (Freud, 1921, 1923), the child soon finds out that he or she is not everything for the mother, except virtually. However, maternal subjectivity harbours a great expectation of absolute coincidence which, when unfulfilled, contributes to impregnating the maternal experience with feelings of inadequacy that we frequently observe in our clinical work.

Special interest should be given to the relations of power-dominance that develop in the intersubjective mother/child space, which signal the force of the identifying enunciates in play. *This develops in the frame of a double asymmetry: on the one hand that of the power ascribed to the mother; on the other hand that of the asymmetry of gender ideals which are being conveyed to the boy and the girl with all the power of the maternal enunciates.*

In this context a field of perceptions, feelings and body contact is organized and an erogenous condition is configured which is different for boys and girls. It includes the way the mother invests her own female body and her daughter's, which will be re-marked by the paternal gaze. The mother differentiates the genders, and the maternal unconscious conveys enunciates regarding the conditions for the development of sexual desire for the boy or the girl. In addition, spaces are delimited for all that is intimate or secret, and maternal identifications are established for the girl, supported by the relational capacities and emotions arising in this "continuity" with respect to the mother.

Both the boy and the girl can represent a phallic value and both can be retained by the mother. But the push towards separation tends to occur more forcefully for the boy, while on the other hand there is greater acceptance of the "naturalness" of continuity and ties with the daughter. The girl will mostly be the mother's double; on the other hand, the boy can be considered as an other, sometimes simply because he belongs to the opposite gender.

Separation as an experience of differentiation from the object is a cut-off that prefigures the recognition of the other as well as of incompleteness in a symbolic sense. *The capacity to produce combinations of unity / separation / symbolic cut-off depends on the insertion of the parents in a symbolic field, and this factor will be decisive in the process of constructing subjectivity beyond gender stereotypes.* These ideas describe the complex conditions in which these variables function in the individual's singularity and how they are re-defined by each personal phantasy.

Towards a plural conception of maternity

What relation is there between the Oedipal girl who wishes to get a child from her father and maternity in a woman? It is important to stress that the emphasis on categorizing the maternal from the perspective of the child leaves aside the recognition of the maternal subjectivity in a relational perspective. *The need to recover or create areas of subjectivity requires recognition of an erotic and non virginal maternity coexisting with a narcissistic and sensual maternity, structuring and loving, and with a tender maternity supported by aim-inhibited drives. But it also means recognizing a non-maternal, non hysterical, sexually erotic femininity.*

Some theories accentuate the fusional and mirrored characteristics of the mother-child dyad; the existence of an archaic *jouissance* not marked by the signifier is also highlighted. *However, a plural conception of maternity must contemplate diverse coexisting planes and recognize that the mother-child intersubjective space is not only mirrored, symbiotic and jouissant, but is in itself a third space.*

Helene Rouch, interviewed by Luce Irigaray (1992), points out that mother/child relations through the placenta, which are presented in the imaginary as a fusion, are in fact "strangely ordered and respectful of the lives of both". Viewing these concepts in metaphoric terms, we could say that the placenta is then more a mediating and regulating system than an element of fusion and lack of differentiation. This also generates the question as to whether separation is an exclusively traumatic condition or whether it includes a pleasurable element.

These ideas are aimed at recognizing the symbolizing, creative capacities in the mother-child space: a concept of a maternity able to promote the child's autonomy and separation, which aims to establish the bases of a symbolic, third function. It means recognizing the child's otherness and renouncing narcissistic wishes of prolongation in the child, thus configuring the foundation for a symbolic cut-off.

Redefining the maternal in relation to femininity also involves redefining masculinity and broadening the concept of paternity to include not only the metaphor of a third party function which separates the mother-child dyad, but also eroticizing and loving aspects, mirrored and caregiving functions which are habitually split off from paternity. Further, it implies the need to explain certain aspects of the maternal which are split off from masculinity because of its threatening quality, but whose recovery as a symbolic category could be the theoretical basis for contemplating aspects linked to the maternal in men today. It also means considering the maternal in a broader perspective than maternity in women. In this regard, I underscore that neither maternity nor paternity should be limited to the child, but both should also generate areas of novel experiences.

These ideas lead me to conceptualize the maternal as a plural experience in an intersubjective dimension; as an experience of coexistence: nature/ culture, body/language, imaginary/symbolic, ego/object, object /other /Other, love/hate, love/aggressiveness. From Nature to the drive, from the drive to the representation, from narcissism to the object, from the ego to the Other, from subject to subject, in a concatenation of connections that transcend binary options and excluding polarities.

The category of maternity, both in its theoretical dimension and as an experience, needs to be de-constructed in regard to its equivalences, isomorphism and conjunctions. It needs to be disconnected from female subjectivity, which amply exceeds it. *In this sense, the woman = mother equation tends to block anxieties referring to sexual difference, otherness and the existence of a non-maternal sexuality in women.* My suggestion is to think of maternity as a multiple configuration, a meeting point for non-exclusive fields, where new forms of symbolic connection must be found which should be able to redefine the relation between maternity and femininity in an expanded complexity. This should allow us to elucidate the relations between motherhood and new reproductive techniques.

The crisis of symbolic references at the turn of the century, the creation of unprecedented forms of filiation, as well as the impact of the presence of changing and uncertain bodies, loosen certainties and attack the symbolic universe. However, they also create conditions which enable us to ask new questions and eventually to reconstruct or construct new symbolic systems of representation.

CHAPTER EIGHT

Femininity and desire

S ubject and desire are two categories whose encounter in the field of femininity is conflictive. Female subjectivity questions its relation with the field of desire; the itineraries of desire in women still traverse imprecise territories.

The naturalist, complementary notions of sexuality signal a limit which is difficult to resolve. Masculine and feminine are polarities sustained throughout the ages, upholding significations regarding forces and principles considered basic for existence. However, these are debatable notions, both because of their strict dichotomy and because of the relative weights that their determinations (biological, psychological, socio-cultural) receive in the different theories. In addition, the categories of woman and the feminine are not equivalent and yet develop complex interrelations. Proposals to think in terms analogous to the masculine only hinder the development of these notions. Work with both concepts means separating them while also sustaining their relations and conflicts.

The transgressive character of desire encounters specific pitfalls in the feminine field. While desire is heavily invested in masculine domains, for women its development is conflictive. Its expression and visibility conflict with narcissistic investments. Relations to beauty and the body image, elements that arouse desire, deserve a space. The values of images and forms (through clothing and make-up as signs that can indicate desire in activity) can become—with the passing of time and physical decline—signs of decadence and the undesirable. In these circumstances the body appears to be something strange, not only for the other but for the subject herself. This may generate experiences of fright or confrontation with the unknown, loss of limits and depersonalization. It is especially important in women because of the progressive extinction of what is currently considered essential to occupying the position of object of desire. Thus desire is experienced as something discordant, while the body and its decline seem to be an "other", a stranger to the individual. In the field of philosophy, Trías (1982) points out the fragile boundaries and easy slips from beauty to the uncanny. Representations of the wife-mother or the virgin-mother as the counterpart of these experiences tend to attenuate them.

When female desire develops as desire for the Other, it can generate the spectre of "lack" in the masculine phantasm; it is a confrontation with sexual difference and otherness which, by de-centring a comfortable complementary relation between the subject and the object of desire, can be manifested in the male as castration anxiety. In these circumstances the proximity of the all-powerful mother imago constitutes a threat to his narcissistic integrity and brings the subject close to the frontiers of the incestuous.

About the non-complementary character of desire

Conceptualizations of women and the feminine are based on a series of premises: theories postulated by anthropology concerning the exchange of women (Lévi-Strauss, 1949) and the position as object of desire are intimately related.

In the psychoanalytic field, Freud (1923) defined, as we have pointed out, a series of elements inherent in the masculine and in the feminine. He associates the masculine with the active, the possession of the penis and the position of subject. He relates the feminine to the passive, the vagina and the position of object. Freud is precise regarding these delimitations which uphold a complementary adequacy between the sexes, both from the biological perspective and from the viewpoint of their respective psychological positions. Although this is an interesting description of the facts and ideas of his times, its consequences create theoretical impasses and have repercussions on clinical work. Is it also Freud's position as a subject of desire? This brings up the problem of the relations between the individual phantasm and the theoretical notions that emerge in the domains of thought. However, we do remember that when Freud develops his conceptions on the Oedipus-castration complex, though it generates a different type of obstacle in the field of the feminine, he proposes an asymmetry between the sexes and detaches his theory from any exclusively naturalist determination of sexual difference.

We have also said that the passive position implies activity because it is included in the drive field and therefore is always active. Freud defined the drive as always active, even though its aim may be passive (1915). Passivity has also been differentiated from receptivity. In the course of his works, Freud (1917, 1930) warns us that activity cannot be mistaken for masculinity and passivity for femininity, showing that it is easy to assimilate these categories too lightly. He emphasizes that the Oedipus complex involves both active and passive positions, in boys as well as in girls. Feminine and masculine are no longer notions attached only to women and men respectively, a strong argument in his discussions. His theory affirms that masculine and feminine are theoretical constructions whose uncertain contents are neither stable nor primary givens. However, he insists that girls must assume passivity if they are to reach femininity, so that in this regard he never abandons the idea that men and women are ultimately complementary.

All these questions converge on an old discussion about the concept of libido: is it masculine or neutral? Freud (1925) refers to one libido—with active and passive aims—which, he affirms, is masculine in the sense that it is active. But he goes on to say (1935) that properly speaking it has no gender, and only could be considered masculine in the conventional sense of equating masculine to active. This clarification is overlooked by most references to this question. The assimilation of concepts such as subject of desire/masculine/active or object of desire/feminine/passive may be significant only in a certain order of logic and discourse, but these slips also embody substitutions that jeopardize our understanding of intersubjective relations on the plane of sexuality.

There is a debatable tendency to associate desire in the feminine field with desire in hysteria. Melman (1985) distinguishes the two when he points out the difference between upholding desire and keeping it unsatisfied. He also emphasizes that the hysterical phantasm maintains that "there is just one sex", an imaginary belief

also shared by masculine phantasms. He adds that there is a temptation to respond from the place of the Master: this would equate
hysteria and femininity, thus denying the latter its own symbolic
support.

Therefore, we underscore that the desired subject differs from the
object of lack. In this sense the desire to be desired is active and is
part of the position of the subject of desire. We also need to differentiate the passivity which can sometimes intervene in both partners
in a mutual play of seduction from the passivity corresponding to
primordial experiences with the primary object.

The position of object of desire, either in women or in men
who place themselves in this position, is part of a series of chains.
In this position the passive predominates: being looked at. This
generates conditions of greater fragility, tending to debilitate and
inevitably leading to relations of subjection. We recall that Aulagnier
(1967) points out that this position can slip with few obstacles into
phantasms of prostitution associated with a desire for anonymity.
These successive slips encourage the masochistic position constructed
on the basis of these phantasms. We stress the inter-crossing of the
drive with power relations in the construction of this position.

We certainly see that the position of object of desire in the domain
of hysteria generates complex and interchangeable power relations.
Thus, passivity may also determine potent effects of domination. At
the same time, this position is associated with the unfathomable and
mysterious quality attributed to the feminine. Veils, masks and
disguises all point to the object of desire whose core is ambiguous
and unknowable. *From this perspective, the position of object of desire
guarantees a certain circulation of the circuit of desire, albeit through the
inclusion of the feminine in the (masculine) universe of the One.*

In Freud's works there are few explanations with regard to desire
in the feminine field beyond maternity. Girls are expected to resolve
their penis envy through the desire for a child, first from their father
and then, in an exogamic resolution, from another man. In these
theorizations, cultural inclusion in a network of social ties develops
through the desire for a child, which makes what would otherwise
remain in the realm of enigma susceptible to representation and able
to acquire a positive condition. In these postulations, no space is left
for developing an itinerary of desire beyond the desire for a child.
In addition, the limits between the paternal function and the libidinal

father are imprecise for the girl, and they are unmarked by prohibition in the strict way they are for the boy, so that they cannot symbolically legalize a "geography of desire" for women.

According to Freud (1917a), inclusion in the field of desire through maternity occurs by means of a chain of equation substitutions. From faeces to penis, from penis to a child, a series of equivalences constructs a road, fated to find symbolic substitutes for a primordial lack. These substitutions indicate an inevitable vicissitude of feminine desire. Although Freud points out that we must distinguish desire for a man from desire for a child, he never fully developed these points. Therefore, in Freudian theory, heterosexual desire is configured in women through the oedipal story, guided by penis envy. But we find that rather than heterosexual desire, it is desire for a child.

Torok (1964) stressed that penis envy is envy of the idealized penis, as a proposal to highlight the original grounding of this concept. The detachment of penis from phallus is an attempt to disconnect these categories from their phallocentric implications. But the apparently neutral concept of phallus as a signifier of desire has unavoidable connotations.

We therefore find two orders of problems. The first is that these developments exclude the possibility of categorizing desire in the field of femininity, except with reference to the desire for a child. The second is that the desire for a child is in itself an equation desire: a substitute for an "original lack". In this context, the question is whether any non-phallic desire is possible, even beyond the most abstract version of the concept of phallus as a signifier of desire in the linguistic field.

Obviously, the concept of desire in psychoanalysis is polysemic. We are moving through areas with diverse, intercrossing significations: from unconscious repressed desire to conscious or preconscious desire, and from unconscious desire to the field of desire exchanges between subjects. One of Freud's most structured definitions is found in "The Interpretation of Dreams" (1900), when he describes unconscious desire in terms of re-establishing the situation of the first satisfaction. In this case, desire is detached from any gender attribution, though its forms of expression are generally sexed. Thus a gap is produced between a non-gender conception of desire and the equations described above, which impress gender on the course of desire.

From lack to productive desire

Subject/object positions in relation to desire are not strictly attached to the masculine or the feminine fields, despite points of predominance, except in the complementary notions of relations between men and women. In the singularity of each subject, more complex options surpass these dichotomies. Equation of these categories with the masculine or the feminine contradicts the concept of position in that it alludes to a phantasm that overflows strict masculine-feminine polarities. *The complexity of the encounter between two subjects, which is always problematic, exceeds the subject/object relationship, and even more so when it is superimposed on fixed significations referring to the masculine or the feminine categories.*

Psychoanalysis generated a great advance when it separated the feminine from being a woman. It enabled "woman" and "feminine" to interplay as two concepts in tension. But psychoanalysis would be severely limited if it ignored their articulations. How do narratives about women influence women and femininity? What is the influence of the real, corporeal fact of being a woman? How does the power of forms come into play? How heavily do the individual phantasms weigh when they converge with or diverge from the above notions? We need to recover both categories: woman and feminine, their indeterminate areas, their relations (not symmetrical with the masculine), as a way to avoid circular explanations.

Shifting the issue from complementary notions of sexual difference to the relation between subjects leads us to work on elucidating which notion of desire we are using. We have stressed that substitute conceptions of desire present two orders of problems: on the one hand they make it difficult to think about feminine sexuality separated from maternity; on the other hand they categorize the desire for a child as a substitute for an "original lack".

These notions are supported by the concept of lack as a previous condition of desire. And lack is conjugated with the phallic function. The phallic order is considered essential to the conception of desire based on an original lack. In this frame, binary systems are indispensable for constructing that logic of desire, since it could only stem from an original lack. This implies that the issue of binary systems is involved in the topic of phallic castration. As we pointed out above, this reasoning inevitably leads to placing women and the feminine in the field of "lack/castration". The concept of symbolic castration comes to our aid in response to this problem, but since this notion applies equally to both sexes in the sense of a metaphorical cut-off which leads to incompleteness and inclusion in a symbolic universe, we also lose the reference to sexual difference. A *productive conception of desire* enables us to displace the question. It does not eliminate the notion of lack but questions its conception as an original and absolute point of departure for the rise of desire, thus opening other options.

We propose to consider two perspectives which enable us to work on different lines and generate potential alternative roads. One perspective is the inclusion of other conceptions of desire which surpass the philosophies of the negative. Nietzsche's ideas generated theoretical currents which enable us to think of desire as production and multiplication. For Deleuze (1980), desire possesses a productive condition *per se*. He postulates that desire is not defined by any essential lack, that the empty spaces and deserts are "fully" part of the field of desire and do not create any kind of lack in it. He considers that "lack refers to a positive condition of desire rather than desire to a negative condition of lack".

When we categorize desire as production, we make it possible to detach the strict equations of subject of desire for the masculine and object of desire for the feminine. It allows us to think about female sexuality neither as mirrored by masculine sexuality nor in terms of a masculine subject of knowledge whose theories are derived only from its own experiences. This creates conditions for de-centring the complementary and also the supplementary conceptions from the feminine centred on the masculine. It also assumes revising the frequent equation between the feminine, the object of desire and "lack". The phallic cover on the object of desire does not exclude this equation; on the contrary, it is inherent in it.

Experiences of love are supported by the interplay between subject of desire and desired object, but the poietic concept of desire breaks up potential stabilization in positions absolutely associated with either the feminine or the masculine. *A productive and positive notion of desire enables us to illuminate singularities in the field of subjectivity, beyond rigid gender assignments in terms of passive-active or subject-object polarities. The relationship between two subjects in the field of sexuality exceeds strict dualities.*

This revision also involves going beyond substitution equations. The symbolic equation indicates a "fate" for the girl in which the desire for a child is the only road to insertion in a symbolic field. This equation has no space for developing an itinerary of desire outside maternity or for the child to be anything more than a substitute for a basic "lack". The equation conception implies repetition; in contrast, the concept of desire as production generates difference. In these conditions, the object of desire becomes a subject. *The encounter between two subjectivities is also an encounter between two mutually heterogeneous others.*

These postulations include traversing the established modes in relationships between men and women, but also an option to go beyond them and surpass strict dichotomous oppositions. Consequently, going through the plane of lack is inevitable, but it is insufficient to explain the complex development of the field of desire.

The notion of lack confronts the subject with an ontological problem which is debated in the field of philosophy. In the psychoanalytic field, it is distinguished from the Freudian concept of lost object as the trigger of desire in relation to the primary object, which removes the illusion of returning to Paradise Lost. We perceive that this object can only be categorized as lost after it has been invested. *Absence must be constituted.* This means that the relation with the object is complex: it is invested and lost at the same time. This also differs from the concept of incompleteness, which signals the access to a symbolic order in terms of contact with finitude, difference and limits. There is no self-sufficient All, and the construction of subjectivity is affected by this fact. There is a disparity between an infinite demand and its necessarily partial and temporary satisfaction.

The notion of lack alone cannot explain the potential to generate difference, since it corresponds to the plane of repetitive insistence. In this sense the concept of original lack, being radical, is inherent in the field of repetition. We therefore postulate that the field of desire develops in two co-existing dimensions, each of which is insufficient by itself to explain the complexity of its configuration. Thus we propose to redefine desire at the intersection between lack and production, between repetition and difference. This way of thinking means accepting the co-existence of different strata concerning subjectivity in terms of non-homogeneous categories.

If desire is no longer only a substitution equation, it dismantles a natural order and an order of equivalences, while also pointing beyond the object. Desire as production is a factor which implies mutations and forked roads, generating potential for aperture and singularity. This poietic function displaces the serial character of equivalences. It leads us to find valid alternative fields that function as bridges between heterogeneous options. It also enables us to think more precisely about the production of difference itself.

A conception of desire that overflows the notion of original lack does not exclude the efficacy of dualistic operations of presence/absence in the genesis of symbolic thought and its representations in the field of infantile sexuality, but encompasses them in plural and complex organizations. By including this conception in a set related to others, we can disassemble strict equivalences which are firmly fixated in shared male and female phantasms as well as in sexual and love relationships.

Another perspective de-centres the concept of desire generated on the basis of lack: that of *imaginary production.* A deeply imaginary dimension of human sexuality is essentially creative, not merely the expression of the suture of an original lack. Although desire is always involved in the process of symbolic representation, the innovative and productive character of the imaginary realm is accentuated in this process.

Castoriadis (1990) shows us the need to include the notion of "radical imagination", with its capacity for creation and transformation, on the individual and social levels. We emphasize that these aspects take shape in each subject through identifications and ideals. The imaginary and symbolic orders are intertwined. From a different vantage point, Winnicott (1959) considered that an absolute disjunction between the imaginary, symbolic and real aspects of experience is unnecessary.

Examination of the imaginary dimensions operating in the symbolic categories also involves reconsidering the equivalences between the phallic order, the law-of-the-father and the symbolic. *The question is whether access to a symbolic universe is equivalent to universal subjection to a phallic order, or whether it is feasible to think of other types of access to the symbolic.*

For David-Menard (1997), the way a woman symbolizes the difficulties inherent in her desire are not resolved mainly through the device that has been called castration: the potential for mourning an object of love does not adopt the argument that it is a part of the body which must be lost in order to be able to represent the renouncement of the object. She adds that the disjunction between penis and phallus signals other roads of symbolization, which the phallus cannot shape. This disjunction questions the concept of universality in relation to the phallic order, and this in turn questions a given notion of desire.

In this context we have to point out changes in the symbolic codes legislating social ties. For Tort (1992), certain analytic notions, especially "the law" and "the symbolic", tend to surreptitiously universalize positive, historical contents which are ignored as such. He adds that there is a temptation to consider that universal facts such as the symbolic character of kinship, the prohibition of incest and the differences of sex and generation concord with the prevalence of the father and masculine domination, historic types of relation which are bound to disappear and are already declining. From these ideas it follows that although the concepts of symbolic order and law-of-the-father are, at present, seemingly inseparable and mutually necessary, they should be distinguished. If this does not occur, an equivalence is produced, in the name of a third party, between the law and the law-of-the-father. This leads to the super-imposition of the third party on what it usually represents, so that in this interplay of transferences the law-of-the-father becomes a universal law.

In this frame, women and the feminine are localized outside the symbolic. The question is how to dismantle this proposal in order to recover aspects necessary for symbolic anchoring in the processes of constructing subjectivity in the field of the feminine. That is, how to go beyond the description and justification of the relations between the symbolic order and the law-of-the-father. If we accept symbolic mediations for accessing subjectivity and desire, this does not preclude consideration of their determinations. The presence and multiplication of two or more linked notions, such as the pre-dominance of the phallic order, the paternal law and the access to a symbolic order, are types of symbolic domination that induce *impasses* in the theory.

In this trajectory, we are referring to the search for an ethic to support a truth of desire that exceeds the complementary conceptions of sexual difference as well as the rigid gender attributions in this field. The ethic of truth does not necessarily coincide with the power of a given discourse. In this sense, although the phallic function is effective to describe the discordant and asymmetric character of the relations between men and women, it does not necessarily express a truth regarding desire. That is, it fails to contribute to the understanding of a possible geography of desire in the field of femininity beyond the desire for a child. The phallic order is *one* of the symbolizing strategies concerning the symbolic-imaginary organizations that structure social ties, while also representing relations of power.

These concepts need to be objects of analysis rather than analytic ideals. The symbolic order enables the subject to integrate into a context of social ties—linked to language and kinship structures— but is also impregnated with empirical, contingent and socio-historical elements. In addition, these considerations do not imply the annulment of sexual figures and their differences, but rather the inclusion and understanding of their determinations.

We need processes of de-centring in order to find a third term for a duality, or a fourth term for a triadic organization, and to develop apertures in closed structures. Thinking in these terms involves displacing false options: *neither merely contingent cultural constructions nor axiomatic universals*. The distinctions between these categories find diverse types of relations: the intersubjective in the construction of subjectivity, the unconscious and desire inside social ties; the internal and the external, configured in folds, de-centre false alternatives.

Including the concept of desire as a productive category in addition to the effectiveness of the imaginary dimension in the field of sexuality allows us to dissociate the subject/object logic from the masculine/feminine polarity. It also enables us to conceive desire as potentially more than a mere substitute for a "basic lack". In this effort to delimit concepts, my proposal is to dismantle universal categories and to assign presence to "the event" (*l'événement*) as the only philosophical concept capable of displacing the verb "to be" and the attribute (Deleuze, 1995). *This involves adding other paths to the repetitive inertia inherent in substitution equations that lead to maternal desire in girls. Desire in production, with its potential for generating difference, functions in relations of liaison and opposition with the equating conception of desire. And it enables us to think about other ways to develop this concept in the field of the feminine.*

CHAPTER NINE

Towards a deconstruction of femininity as a universal category

Universal/singular

As we advance through the itinerary of this book, we return to dilemmas we have already formulated but need to examine. Is it possible to sustain a universal conception of women or does the process of access to subjectivity imply thinking in terms of diversities and singularities? This leads to a broader question: do we have to choose? We cannot say that these options are false or that each one does not correspond to certain realities, but if either of them is presented as an absolute, then it does become a fictional discourse. The concept of universal categories aims at conditions of constancy, fixedness and non-temporality on which essentialist conceptions about women are sustained.

Biological essentialism maintains that sexual difference is fundamentally biological and anatomical. It insists that the categories of masculine and feminine are an inevitable consequence of previous data regarding the differential biology of men and women. It ignores the power of phantasy and sexual desire, ignores the historic character of the concepts of sexual difference, and fails to see that they are a construction. It omits any consideration about intersubjectivity. This is the power of essentialism within the biological frame.

Cultural essentialism maintains that sexual difference is determined solely by culture, without considering articulations and intersections with the drive, the unconscious sexual desire and phantasy. This is the power of essentialism within the cultural frame.

The opposition to any fundamental truth concerning the feminine condition means rejecting any type of induction to a model of prefixed femininity. On the contrary, essentialism tends to make sexual difference either "natural" or "cultural", each alternative excluding the other. At the opposite pole, the tendency of eclecticism is to fragmentation or to an indifferent type of thinking, thus diluting the concept of difference itself and the inclusion of the subject in a symbolic order.

Universal notions on women are intimately related to binary thought, which generates an essentialist view for each term of a dichotomy. However, to question essentialist and universal positions does not mean that we ignore the specificities of the masculine and the feminine categories, which also include ambiguities and complexities. The task of complex thinking is to sustain the paradoxes, contradictions and theoretical tensions—as opposed to essentialist notions, whether they belong to the biological or cultural realm—including the historical character of the conceptions on sexual difference as well as the efficacy of the field of desire.

At birth, every human being is placed into one of two fields: the feminine or the masculine. If this nomination is problematic, a conflict ensues. This is a cultural operation that assigns meaning and provides imaginary and symbolic signification to the anatomical sexual difference, which has yet to be symbolized by the infant. This operation is based fundamentally on the power of the forms, which are in turn signified culturally, marking a diversity of genders.

However, we also need to bear in mind that the dualistic concepts of gender have not always been formulated in the same way. In the Aristotelian model, the irreducible character of the opposite sex finds other options. For the ancient Greeks, there were three double beings: man/man, woman/woman and man/woman. There are fusions and dichotomies, unions and mixtures between the feminine and the masculine. The passage from the baroque forms of the mixtures, through the androgyne and the hermaphrodite, to the classical figures of sexual difference reveals changes in the conception of difference in Occidental culture from the Greeks to the present day.

An inter- and trans-subjective horizon marks the consensuses of significations, practices and social bonds of each period. Everyday speech, myths and stories express singularities in sexual practices and in male-female relations. In this frame, transsexualism can be seen as an expression of the uncertainties of sexual identity. It generates a scenario whose representational ambiguity generates anxiety because it attempts to transcend the anatomical difference. To this we may add the ethnic, racial and religious diversities pertaining to different contexts of culture and discourse, which make the feminine a non-homogeneous category. Particular cultures, different original myths and diverse social classes and ethnic groups signal the many ways in which the feminine is imaginarily organized. Thus a number of factors do question the concept of universality in relation to women, in spite of the unquestioned acceptance of traditions, myths, naturalist conceptions and notions of primary identity, which encourage fixed and absolute conceptions of masculinity and femininity.

With regard to the concept of singularity, it can be defined in more than one way. On the one hand, we refer to singularity in relation to individual phantasy. In another perspective, we point out the conceptions of Lacan, who takes the notions of "universal" and "denied universal" within a scheme of logical and philosophical categories modified by him. He emphasizes the contingency and singularity of the feminine position *versus* the universality of the masculine position. These are positions relative to language which are played out around the phallic function. Lacan contributes the idea of singularity regarding the feminine position; however, he also "sexualizes" the categories of universal and contingent, assigning them to the masculine and feminine positions respectively. For this author, women are not in any class and are not inscribed in the universal; they are "excluded from the nature of things, which is the nature of words" (Lacan, 1972–3). This sets them apart from discourse and from the universality of a symbolic determination.

From another perspective, Monique David-Ménard (1997) under-scores some weak and obscure points in the notion of universality. She maintains that when a thought is defined by universality, a wordless act is committed: the erasure of the articulation between phantasy and concept. In this way the universality of the conceptual tool erases the modes of its construction. For this author, the construction of the concept of universality in Kant and other thinkers expresses a masculine anthropology of sexual desire. She therefore proposes re-opening a question which the "philosophies of the universal" close: to sustain a certain contingency of thinking as a position of intermediation.

***

The questioning of an essentialist and universal conception of the feminine and women does not prevent us considering categories held in common by women in general or investigating their genealogies. In this sense, relations of domination and hierarchies indicate collective phenomena which are doubtless present. Enunciates affirming common conditions for a group or class impregnate practices and social discourse, and are a strongly unifying point. Relations of domination involve considering a subject as an object, which weakens whoever occupies this position. These relations produce an isomorphism of the categories of woman and object.

On the other hand, belonging to minority contexts, as women do, can determine very complex power relations, consecrating phenomena that wreak double or triple violence because of their articulation with religious or ethnic contexts. Thus local identities can become, within their boundaries, other ways to homogenize diversities.

***

Although we consider that the category of woman cannot be universalized monolithically, we are not proposing any form of anarchic diversity. In this sense, we do point out both the risks of a universalizing perspective leading to a loss of the singularity of each subject and the risks of singularity as an impediment to theorizing on points in common.

Theories oscillate between the tendency to universalize the categories of man and woman and the opposite, which tends to consider them in their singularity. The former presents the risks of unifying different types of subjectivities and so reinforcing dichotomies. In this sense it involves a reductive position concerning subjectivity. Thus we need to surpass this position, although it is part of accepted social bonds. The latter reinforces the heterogeneous—whatever pertains to each subject—but also implies the risk of ignoring the qualities of a set in the context of a given culture and discourse.

My proposal is to consider the relation of women to the feminine at the intersection between the singular and the universal. The concepts of universality and singularity are not mutually exclusive; each has its own areas as well as broad intersections which can only be categorized through non-disjunctive forms of thought. This means considering common categories as well as others which are diverse and singular, *plus* their co-existence, even including their paradoxes and contradictions. Furthermore, it means considering the possibility of new configurations at these intersections. In this sense we support the search for what is produced *between* categories and dichotomies: between what is neither one nor the other.

Between the singular and the universal, frontier zones are generated. When we go through the universal, we discover common elements in the genealogy of the construction of masculinity and femininity, but this passage should develop the necessary conditions for becoming a subject, which differ with each individual. Between fixed roles and identity stereotypes, the value of phantasy and desire emerges.

The production of subjectivity

We know that references to man or woman are not the same as references to masculinity and femininity, and that these categories come into play in the homosexual or heterosexual object choice in different ways. Since they cannot be unified, we find contradictions in many women between contemporary ideals of femininity and the development of their sexual desire. We also know that any subject can be permeated by phantasies labelled masculine or feminine, independently of their anatomical sex. But, as we have underlined, the question does not end here, since each subject, man or woman—because of their anatomy, assignment of sex and name, identifications and desires—has a different relationship with masculinity and femininity.

In this context, I return to the Freudian proposal in "The Psychogenesis of a Case of Homosexuality in a Woman" (1920), to remind us of other ways of thinking which avoid a linear determinism. Freud considers the various elements that come together in the constitution of a sexed subject: the physical sexual characters, the mental sexual characters—masculine or feminine—and the kind of object-choice, homo- or heterosexual. Freud (1920) says that it is a question of three sets of characteristics "which, up to a certain point, vary independently of one another, and are met with in different individuals in manifold permutations".

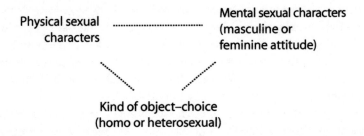

Physical sexual characters .... Mental sexual characters (masculine or feminine attitude)

Kind of object–choice
(homo or heterosexual)

With this proposal, Freud avoids a strictly biologist posture and breaks the tendency to naturalize the sexual difference. The idea emerges of the co-existence of different fields, which may be convergent or divergent; different combinations may develop between identifications and the field of sexual desire and object choice, with asymmetric effects for the masculine or feminine position. The relations between ideal identifications and the field of desire, between the erogenous body and the anatomical body mark multiple crossroads and combinations which transcend any attempt to universalize the processes of constructing subjectivity. The production of subjectivity is singular and cannot be transferred.

The connections between these fields transcend the notion of levels of integration, which imply the possibility of a final synthesis of these planes. On the contrary, we consider that they form relations of conjunction and disjunction, generating conditions of heterogeneity opposed to total integration, although they may include partial integrations. *Thus different levels of organization are formed: the assignation of a sex (which does not always tally with anatomy), the identifying enunciates and the field of desire. These three heterogeneous orders are tied together.* The categorization of these knots requires bridge-theories. This knotting in turn produces different effects on subjectivity depending on their relation either to the line of repression or of disavowal, resulting in different clinical formations.

None of those levels of organization is independent of the *intersubjective field*. In the first place, the body is always an erogenous body, and in this sense is constructed and marked since its initial contact with the primary object. The natural categories are constructed through significations. For this reason it is difficult to speak of a pure biological sex, although *this does not mean that we ignore the material anatomical sexual difference that operates as a limit*. The erogenous body is neither the anatomical body nor the body of need, but is constructed on them. The sexed body is a first fact of material reality that the newborn offers. It is never totally natural, or if it is, its "nature" is a fictional copy of the natural. The body's interpreted or constructed character implies that both male and female bodies respond to a form, a *Gestalt* that informs language, and also the opposite: that language informs the bodies. The sexed body requires significations; human mediation impresses their marks.

In the second place, we find the level of the identifying ideals concerning femininity and masculinity. This is an imaginary level, which may be concordant or discordant with the ideals proposed by cultural codes.

In the third place we detect the field of the drive and sexual desire. Sexual desire is supported by the drive, but its geography is also generated by the significations that emerge in the intersubjective field.

The discussion on intersubjectivity therefore involves speaking of the psyche as an open system in relation to an Other, beyond essentialist invariants. Intersubjectivity is a mediator of a symbolic world, organized by language and its significations, coexisting with the power of the iconic and the persistence of myths. *Therefore, other vectors are articulated: the drive, the iconic, the heterogeneous Other and symbolic thirdness.*

Construction/Deconstruction

Our proposal discusses the need for processes of *construction and deconstruction*, whose elements operate through relations of multiplicities. This conception contributes an anti-essentialist view: to be a man or a woman is neither a natural determination nor an irreversible fact, but a construction in which anatomy may or may not coincide with masculinity or femininity, and these variables may in turn not coincide with the itineraries of sexual desire. I use the concept of deconstruction in order to question relations postulated as fixed and essential. This makes it possible for us to unravel fictions and crystallized concepts as well as conventions and norms. *It allows us to question whether there is any "essential" truth about sexual desire or sexual identity, considering that femininity unseats a certain comfort in regard to the knowledge of sexual difference.* The possibilities of deconstructing fixed significations assigned to the genders and undoing stereotypes of the masculine and the feminine positions contribute a factor of relativism and historical perspective which questions substantialist conceptions on the subject.

Deconstruction aims to investigate the ways discourses circulate, in an attempt to disarm a hegemonic way of thinking which can only apply to a closed system. But at the same time we need to consider another aspect of deconstruction which relativizes any notion of truth. By rejecting any conception of a subject whatsoever, even a split subject, it denies any possibility of binding in the frame of Eros. *Therefore, deconstruction is a necessary but not a sufficient exercise; its contribution to undoing absolutist discourses should promote the construction of new significations.* In this sense, constructions involve a potential for psychic re-inscriptions and the remodelling of phantasies.

***

Feminine subjectivity is formulated in a context of conflicting options: between the difficult access to subjectivity for women in Modernity and the postmodern dissolution of the subject, new challenges are constantly generated. The notions concerning the relation between the subject and the feminine have been articulated only recently and with considerable conflict. In this sense, we need to stress that the postmodern annihilation of the subject can lead to abstractions of text and discourse. At the same time, the insufficiencies of the phallic order are evident—even its most abstract level in the signifying field—for understanding and theorizing on the feminine. We underscore the need to include other types of logic and other conceptions, neither complementary nor symmetric with the masculine, nor substantial, which should allow us to include binary thought as an inevitable passage to other, more encompassing options.

We propose the relations between women and the feminine as a configuration which responds to continuities and discontinuities. The continuities are organized as regularities which take shape in a space and a time, and in a relationship with an Other, within the inter-subjective frame. The discontinuities attack any homogeneous and unitary concept of identity, questioning the universal conception of women and clashing with the postulate of a feminine essence in several perspectives: *first,* because of the existence of an individual phantasy that cannot be transferred, *second,* because of identifying diversities, *third,* because of the potential discontinuities between anatomical sex and gender ideals, and *fourth,* because of the intrusion of unconscious sexual desire as a discordant factor.

This implies salvaging the concept of subjectivity, which avoids homogenizing the categories of the feminine or the masculine, including the power of phantasy and the singularity of each individual. Access to subjectivity involves unfastening the universals in relation to sexual difference. The construction of singularity reveals that sexuality exceeds the categories of masculinity and femininity, although its relation with them is complex. *But at the same time, the production of subjectivity does not exclude its articulation in a field of specificities pertaining to trans-subjective and intersubjective fields, which have powerful and doubtless efficacy. In this sense, access to subjectivity is an exercise of multiplicities. Between the sexed bodies, the gender beings and the subjects of sexual difference, frontier zones are configured which mutually touch and overlap. Subjects emerge which are neither unified nor can they be unified, because of their constitutive heterogeneity.* At the edges, these categories articulate or collide; a different field develops which is not the same as the original one, and it makes other levels of psychic construction possible.

CHAPTER TEN

Between sex and gender: the paradigm of complexity

Throughout recent decades, many changes have taken place in relations, both private and public, between men and women, though partial and unequally distributed among the population. We have also seen many contributions to the theories which explain these changes. In this context, two conceptions concerning sexual difference coexist today in the field of culture. On the one hand, Modernity defined two strictly differentiated spaces, the masculine and the feminine, upholding their radical difference. On the other hand, the turn of the century has seen the emergence of a multiplicity of sexual and gender variants which attempt to challenge the concepts of Modernity on sexual difference and upset any given legality regarding genders. These phenomena are not new, but do acquire special resonance because of the advances of biotechnology, because they have gained increased social acceptance and have been spread by the mass media. Frequently, neither the emitter nor the receptor can differentiate between homosexuality, transsexualism, transvestism or bisexuality, since they often seem to be interchangeable. These sexual migrations accompanying the phenomenon of Postmodernity organize narratives which may ultimately result in a disorganized and indifferent enumeration of variants and particularities of sexual practices, thus diluting concepts in relation to the symbolic structuring of a subject.

As we have already pointed out, these presentations are far from novel. In the Middle Ages, mixed figures such as female Christs or breast-feeding Christs questioned the classical binary system of sexual difference. From the double, androgynous beings described by Plato to the shamanic phenomena of trance and transformation into the other sex; from the Italian mystical poets of the Stilnovo in the 13th century, who called themselves women, to the lamas who identified, through a hallucinatory trance, with their goddesses, there is a nearly infinite series of processes of transformations, fusions and identifications between the masculine and the feminine (Zolla, 1981). These processes also occur in Tantra, Taoism and Buddhism. Both of these tendencies now co-exist: the strict separation of the sexes in Modernity and the sexual variants that Postmodernity has ushered in. They are part of the consensuses of significations of a period, on a horizon of historiographies which support a group of practices in social relations.

In this context, we propose the possible relations and eventual oppositions between psychoanalytic theories and gender theories. I will approach this subject from two angles: firstly, the concept of gender and the sex-gender system: its meaning, theoretical and clinical interest and its debatable points; and secondly, the psycho-analytic perspective on sexual difference and its theoretical-clinical implications as well as its areas of debate. In these discussions, we also recognize that neither of these two fields offers a unified or homogeneous theory on these issues, but only theoretical pre-eminences.

Gender

The concept of gender originates in the field of social sciences and is applied today in disciplines such as anthropology, philosophy and psychology. It postulates that femininity and masculinity are categories which respond to a cultural construction. This concept is used mainly by Anglo-Saxon scholars and very little by the French. Historically, it responds to different needs: on the one hand, to find theoretical instruments to understand the hierarchic relations between the sexes and phenomena of violence in this connection; and on the other hand it provides explanations of such growing phenomena as transsexualism and transvestism in relation to the concept of sexual identity.

Gender studies replace the studies on women which were in vogue in the sixties, when it was women who were the object of study. This replacement was an attempt to de-centre the category of women as an object of analysis or investigation, because it carried a double connotation: first, that the female condition was a problem; second, that a subject of knowledge, neutral and exterior to that field, might be possible. Therefore, categories referring to the masculine were introduced.

A broad field of study began to grow. Among other issues, conceptions, myths, stereotypes and roles which are welded either to masculinity or to femininity were examined. These included on the one hand conceptions of virility in connection to figures such as Don Juan or the macho; and on the other hand conceptions of femininity in which women appear as embodying contradictory figures: either a depository of dangerous, uncontrolled sexuality or a pure, virginal and asexual being. Other lines emphasize the sexed character of language, questioning its supposed neutrality (Fox Keller, 1994). This author points out that language includes the concept of gender, which encompasses a set of beliefs organized as myths, making them unquestionable.

However, although gender studies attempt to de-centre from women as an object of study, we all find that in general the concept of gender does refer to women. We also know that gender studies are not univocal. Some lines emphasize the concept of equality between genders. Others accentuate the difference between them. Some try to assign a positive value to certain characteristics attributed to femininity which have traditionally been considered negative (emotions, sensitivity, capacity for caregiving). Other tendencies distinguish precisely that equality does not cancel out the sexual difference.

The sex/gender system

The sex/gender system, introduced by G. Rubin (1975) for anthropology, is a formulation that aims to disarticulate sex and gender. In this proposition, sex refers to anatomy—sex in the biological sense—while gender is considered a cultural construction which signals and gives significations to anatomical sex. This conception implies de-centring away from the biological and the naturalist conceptions. We can relate it to the well-known thesis of Simone de Beauvoir (1949) that "women are made, not born". This affirmation questions the essentialist conceptions of an "eternal feminine", natural and substantial.

Stoller (1984) considers the strength of cultural determinants which, in the frame of primary relations, mark the child from birth through the first gender-related identifications. In his studies on transsexualism, and referring to a paper by Money and the Hampsons (1957), he works with the concept of sex/gender dissociation when he tries to explain the pre-eminence of the sense of belonging to a gender in spite of anatomy. He postulates the existence of three planes: core gender identity, gender identity and gender roles. The core gender identity is pre-oedipal, constituted in a non-conflictive way, and once established, is unmovable after the age of two and a half. For this author, masculinity or femininity is determined primarily by culture and responds to post-natal learning. These conceptualizations involve several issues that we need to address:

1. Although it contributes elements for examining the beliefs that support the conviction of belonging to a masculine or feminine field, the core of gender identity appears to be a major, unquestionable articulator.
2. This context accentuates that for some schools of thought, psychosexuality emerges as a consequence of this major articulator.
3. The concept of identity, if categorized as something equal to itself, must be reconsidered, since it is a key concept in these theorizations.
4. The sex/gender system contributes elements for disarticulating gender identity from the biological factor. However, an insufficiently explored field concerning their potential and complex relations remains open.

Today, gender theories themselves include a broad area of debate. These are some of the controversial points: firstly, the concept of gender tends to universalize categories referring to the masculine and the feminine, focusing either on equality or difference. In this aspect it cannot avoid the risks of binary systems. It has also been pointed out that this universality concerning gender categories involves other risks: they may be "naturalized", and consequently ignore the value of the phantasm in each subject. Nevertheless, some authors (Butler, 1990) maintain that important cultural, religious, ethnic, racial and social class differences mean that women's problems cannot be compared or universalized. Yet, other lines point out the importance of gender theories for explaining the phenomena of violence, domination and social inequality between genders, based on the study of the legitimization and prescription of roles.

Another issue being debated is that some theoretical currents propose a pre-subjective, pre-symbolic, biological sex, which later receives a gender mark by culture. But other theories consider biological sex itself a construction which is signified by the concepts of difference inherent in the trans-subjective field. In this sense, biological sex would also be secondary (Laqueur, 1990). For this author, previous notions of difference and identity determine what is seen and said concerning the body.

Thirdly, Laplanche (1980) questions the sex-gender system's placement of one term in the area of anatomy and the other in the area of psychology. He postulates that it is best to use the term sex for the set of physical or psychic determinations, behaviour and phantasms which are directly linked to the sexual function and pleasure; and the term gender for the set of physical or psychic determinations, behaviour and phantasms which are linked to the masculine/feminine distinction.

In this review, we find that the concept of gender is a category supported by determinations of the universes of discourse, language and socio-culture. In this context, the notion of gender identity refers to the imaginary structuring of the ego and the correlate given ideals on masculinity and femininity.

From psychoanalysis

In general, the concept of gender is not included in the theoretical corpus of psychoanalysis. However, psychoanalysis was born as a result of Freud's encounter with hysterical patients: problems of sexual desire and repression which he used as a model of the psychic apparatus—but, in addition, problems regarding predominantly the feminine gender.

Although there is no strict relation between a given gender and specific clinical configurations, we do find predominance. We could consider this predominance as relating to the position, masculine or feminine, of each subject, which goes beyond gender. However, rather than eliminating the question of the incidence of these clinical configurations in one position or the other, it only displaces the problem.

We cannot ignore the higher incidence of certain depressions in women; for example, those related to the crises of the middle stages of life. Nor can we ignore the fact that today we observe eating disorders, such as the anorexia-bulimia pairing, mainly in young women. Similarly, we find addictions more frequently in men. It is interesting to observe how the body can be transformed into a means of expression which, however, is different from the scenario of hysteria. The symptom as a symbolic expression of conflict yields its place to the body as an effect of what cannot be symbolized.

Eternal youth and beauty emerge as narcissistic mandates which are heavily accentuated at the turn of the century. In a context where certain postmodern tendencies express loss of values and fall of ideals, those ideals emerge in contrast with maximum value for women and, with a show of exacerbated narcissism, also extend to men. We have to question how these mandates are expressed and passed down through identifying and imaginary enunciates—whose efficacy is indubitable—that impregnate the intersubjective mental space in which the newborn relates to its primary objects. Bodily transgressions express a questioning of these identifying enunciates that cannot be refuted and are therefore thrown out of the symbolic field.

We also need to consider another topic in relation to the masculine or feminine, which is paternity or maternity. Half a century ago, Marie Langer (1951) already observed a specific problem: when women's inevitable fate was maternity, there was a concomitant increase in hysteria and repressed sexuality. Later on, when maternity stopped being a unique and inexorable fate, women who were not mothers began to be protagonists and to enjoy greater sexual and social freedom. This author points out that in these new conditions, hysteria and sexual repression decreased, while psychosomatic and functional disorders of the maternal functions grew more frequent. We stress that this could be related to the strict splitting between maternity and feminine sexuality. In addition, we should consider the fact that in the frame described by Langer, maternity is losing its facilitated symbolic access and thus becoming a problematic issue. In addition, maternity is currently still basically a matter for women and paternity for men, these roles being assigned traditionally to a specific gender. However, the new subjectivities emerging at the intersection of Modernity and Postmodernity challenge these parameters. The new reproductive techniques and new types of families and couples form configurations which question these fixed roles, just as transsexualism challenges the power of anatomical determinations.

Psychoanalytic theories

In the field of psychoanalysis, there is no single perspective on sexual difference or on the concepts of masculinity and femininity. Freud's works are also multifocal in this sense, and we will therefore discuss one of his dominant lines of thinking. For Freud (1925), as we said before, it is the resolution of the Oedipus-castration complex and access to sexual difference that allows each subject to place him- or herself in a masculine or feminine position. This means that the little boy gives up the primary object, which is usually the mother, and identifies with the father; this is the condition for his sexual desire to turn to exogamic substitute objects of love. In this way, the child accesses a norm governed by the prohibition of incest, which involves insertion in a context of social bonds.

This refers to boys; for girls he describes a more complicated itinerary. In this sense, we cannot ignore the fact that for Freud, the subject around which the theory of the Oedipus complex and access to sexual difference is organized was originally masculine; or that women, though they had a part in the origins of his conceptions on hysteria and the psychic apparatus, were subsequently placed in a constellation that provoked debate from the outset.

These ideas imply that placement in one category or the other, masculine or feminine, is a consequence of the oedipal resolution, meaning that it is secondary. In this view, anatomy would no longer be the main determinant of sexual difference, although we are aware of Freud's fluctuations on this point. He de-centres but does not annul anatomical determinations; instead, they integrate a series of complex articulations which cannot be reduced to any single determination.

We recall that Freud modified his theoretical position in relation to women and sexual difference. The Freudian positions began by oscillating between the analogies and the symmetries between the sexes. He later abandoned the concept of any kind of parallelism or symmetry, but preserved the idea of an ultimate complementary relation. The girl had to follow a complicated road—starting with an original masculinity—to become the necessary complement for the male. That is to say he starts from an asymmetric prototype only to reach a complementary adaptation, on the basis of a naturalist model.

On the other hand, theories of object relations accentuate the child's initial relations with the primary object, the mother, and posit a primary femininity. For his part, Winnicott (1966) proposes a primary femininity for both sexes, referring to primary identifications at the level of being and existence. Therefore, this author considers it important to recover feminine aspects, usually split off in men to avoid an attack on their masculinity, which originate in primordial, pre-drive moments.

This thinking shows us another tendency that describes how the subject takes elements called masculine or feminine into his or her constitution as such. We can also deduce that the anxiety provoked by the feminine, which Freud postulated for both sexes, would be related to these primordial moments. However, for Lacan, the subject, always divided, is the result of a linguistic operation, of which the subject is an effect. Placement in a masculine or feminine position depends on the relation with the phallic function and *jouissance* (1972–73).

Faure-Oppenhemier (1980) maintains that theories on sexual identity emphasize the role of gender and the assignment of sex, while minimizing their physical anchoring. This author considers that there is a tendency to give priority to gender over the body. She thinks that the sexed body is indispensable for configuring gender, specifying that the drive cathects the gender, while gender creates conditions for emergence of the drive.

Gender identity and sexual difference

In a broad sense, we could say that psychoanalysis also includes a gender theory, although its significations imply different conse-quences for the theory. For some psychoanalytic schools of thought, gender theories are sociological theories which are extraneous to the psychoanalytic field. They therefore consider that the issue should centre on access to sexual difference through the resolution of the Oedipus-castration complex. For others, the gender factor acts in the culture into which the baby is born, and operates through ideals and stereotypes it prescribes for each gender.

Gender Theories	Psychoanalytic Theories (Freudian)
Gender Identity	Sexual Difference
Pre–Oedipal	Oedipal
Current masculine or feminine ideals	Psycho–sexuality and object choice

These positions include the debate concerning the access to sexual difference through oedipal resolution versus the constitution of a core of gender identity in the pre-oedipal field.[1] *However, we see that we are considering different categories. Gender identity focuses on one perspective and sexual difference on another.*

The concept of *identity* is controversial in the psychoanalytic field. It refers to a sense of continuity, to the structuring of the self, to forms that configure an ego. It inevitably has a core of ambiguity. The notion of primary and essential identity encourages fixed and essential conceptions of masculinity and femininity. However, we have to consider that sexual identity is assigned at birth and places the newborn in the field of either the masculine or the feminine, as an imaginary configuration with ulterior effects of truth. Through maternal discourse, the identifying project (Castoriadis-Aulagnier, 1975) inevitably contains significations and enunciations in this sense. The phantasms relating to the primary scene and the four positions of the Oedipus complex further complicate that initial assignment.

These points of view question the concept of identity as a fixed category, unquestionable and immutable, which tends to naturalize the difference. The subject has no identity in a logical sense, as an equivalent to itself, except in the field of repetition and regarding the absolutism of the ideal ego. At the narcissistic centre of the ideals, the ideal ego outlines a horizon of totality: the One, a "true", stable, homogeneous and universal identity. In this sense, if primary identity were a major articulator structuring the psyche, it would produce an indifferent co-existence of sexual and gender variants, with no understanding of their relations with the symbolic universe and the field of psychosexuality.

The formation of the ego ideal, post-oedipal and situated in a symbolic frame, limits the absolutism of the One. There are no fixed, absolute or eternal ideals. Could we therefore think in terms of an exploratory aspect of the so-called identity categories, which we can thus view as not simply defensive and deceitful? Further, if we think of identity in terms of identifications and also think about these identifications in a plural frame, we can categorize a concept of identity beyond repetition, which signals a difference. The power of stereotypes and fixed roles shrinks in the same proportion as the potential for dealing with sexuation symbolically grows. The move from the ideal ego to the ego ideal generates a field which provides a possibility to break with the totality of Unity. These advantages encourage us to think in terms of a complex notion of identity which also involves questioning the concept of universality in the field of the feminine.

Sexuality also exceeds the unitary concept of identity, since it acts as a constant disruptive factor. This creates a core of ambiguity inherent in the identity categories, so that we are obliged to view sexual identity as an effect of a multiplicity of determinations, rather than as an absolute essence. *Knowledge of gender identity can co-exist with ignorance of sexual difference.*

What psychoanalysis propounds, across all its different theoretical lines, is the power of sexual desire, the drive and the phantasms, in the constitution of subjectivity. This implies underscoring all that is singular in each individual, that which cannot be transferred. *Sexual desire always emerges as an excess*: it goes beyond the concept of identity, though it does not cancel it out. On this level, it is important to emphasize that the roads of sexual desire are not arbitrary and that its configurations respond to precise determinations.[2] As we have stressed, this means considering subjectivity as a singularity which cannot be transferred, though involved in relations of conjunction and disjunction with what is inter- and trans-subjective. In other words, we postulate neither pure singularity nor absolute universals.

Trans-subjective, intersubjective and intrapsychic

In this debate, we return to an old controversy with regard to the kind of interaction between two seemingly incompatible elements: on the one hand the intrapsychic, and on the other hand the trans-subjective in a broad sense. *I say "seemingly" because the incompatibility appears when we forget to consider their modes of interrelation, whether concordant or discordant.*

Trans-subjective field	The intrapsychic

Each theory focuses on one or another parameter. My intention is to show that this arrangement forces us to think in terms of mutually excluding, dichotomous operations between the trans-subjective and the intrapsychic. These positions generate a theoretical limit. As I pointed out, my proposal is to consider other types of thinking that allow us to break away from binary options and mutually excluding polarities, and to think in terms of relations which are more logical than causal, and therefore allow us to consider multiplicities. Tort (1992) maintains that the questions of culture and social and historical determinations are not extrinsic to psychoanalysis, nor are they extra-disciplinary. They are also not interdisciplinary but rather intrinsic to psychoanalysis.

Therefore, I return to the opposition between the trans-subjective and the intrapsychic field in order to re-formulate it with the concept of *intersubjectivity*, which allows us to underscore that culture does not act directly or without mediation. The mother/child intersubjective space is a space of mediation and transmission in which trans-subjective discourse is processed by the mother's desires and wishes. It develops in an imaginary register which nonetheless has powerful structuring efficacy. Sexual desires, phantasies and the oedipal structure already present in the parents are actualized in the intersubjective space, but transmission is by no means passive: the adult's sexuality is always present.

Nor is there a pure intrapsychic field: a body sustained on drive is made erogenous by the mother. In this sense, the concept of the intrapsychic is a closed concept which we need to open in order to highlight how the intrapsychic and the drive field are marked out by an Other.

Intersubjectivity	Intrapsychic field
Mother–child, Father–child spaces	Drive: border concept between the somatic and the psychic
Discourse, gazes, contacts, rhythms, language	Representations and affects

If we bring these fields closer together, we see that a shared area or intersection is generated. The concept of an *fold* allows us to avoid false options: internal and external are re-defined in a border space, surpassing the interior/exterior antinomy.

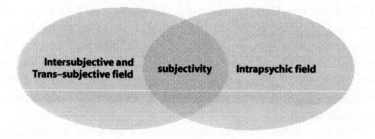

In the intersection, subjectivity is generated as a singular and non-transferable fact which is, however, impregnated with plural universes.

In this network of categories, we must include *relations of power-domination* between genders. The contributions of Foucault (1979) allow us to establish relations, previously invisible, between the concepts of gender, sexuality and power. Foucault also inverts their causal relation. This author considers that power relations constitute sexual desire and sexuality in general, thus including power structurally. The subject is instituted in a network of powers configured as multiple relations of force. Any power relation needs knowledge, on which it does not depend, but which lends it efficacy. Effects of power circulate in identifying enunciates.

At the same time, the organization of knowledge concerning women's bodies expresses relations of power. In the body of hysteria, fascination operates as an element of power over the Other, but can be countered—in a play of opposites—by depreciation, as a factor of counter-power. Also, the idealized body of procreation rests, among other determinations, on an original core: maternal power.

Perspectives on gender impregnate social discourse and are embodied in the form of imaginary identifications in each subject. They also express the relations of power-domination inherent in binary configurations. In this sense, we cannot avoid going through gender dualisms. This passage can help us on the one hand to deconstruct the homogeneous concepts of collective identity, and on the other hand to illuminate the relations of power-domination pertaining to the masculine-feminine, active-passive and phallic-castrated binary systems. This implies that we can operate within gender, not acritically but as one focus in a complexity.

However, we also need to go beyond gender. *Entering and going beyond the perspectives on gender should be seen as an oscillation rather than as a single option.* Each individual accedes to them through identifications, configured in the frame of intersubjectivity. But emergence as a subject involves going beyond gender stereotypes, by dis-identifying from the collective designation. This means thinking about the multiple universes that inhabit subjectivity (Guattari, 1992).

Gender diversity and sexual difference are disjunctive concepts whose mode of relation is complex and not unidirectional. This mode assumes co-existence in tension. When we think in these terms we simultaneously use logics that appear to be contradictory and temporalities that seem to be mutually exclusive. The constitution of subjectivity in a symbolic-imaginary frame travels more complex roads than the binary options, although it includes them on the way. As Pontalis describes it (1982): "concerning the assignment of a sexual identity, an entire lifetime is not too long for each of us to respond personally to the answers presented to us as givens."

Notes

1. cf. Chapter Two in reference to the pre-oedipal stage as a multifocal space, with different significations.
2. cf. Chapter Eight.

CHAPTER ELEVEN

Otherness, diversity and sexual difference

The tendency to consider femininity as a problematic topic derives from the theories concerning the sexual difference. We intend to displace the "problem" of the feminine onto the question of sexual difference. This means we need to move in the opposite direction from the trend that places the issue of sexual difference in women. In this way we attempt to reposition the conditions of this displacement which conceals the enigma of difference behind the so-called enigma of femininity.

We also need to consider that the psychoanalytic field has no unitary theory on sexual difference. This question is formulated in diverse dimensions, and each theoretical current focuses on one which accords with its particular interpretative frame. The points of controversy generated cannot be exempt from the question of whether or not there is a universal and essentialist conception of women. They involve different notions and logic systems about women, the feminine and sexual difference.

A complementary view of the sexual difference oriented towards a reproductive model is not enough to encompass these questions. For Leclaire (1996), the opposition between nature and culture is seen today as an opposition between two different types of symbolic activity. In this sense, it is important to stress that there are ambiguities and intermediate areas between anatomy, identifications and desire as well as between women and the feminine. Therefore, we need to develop this question as a field of support to understand the access to subjectivity.

Re-formulating the logic of the construction of differences may show the way to other conceptual delimitations, in theory and in clinical practice. On the basis of these problems, I will examine the concepts of otherness, heterogeneity, diversity and difference in relation to the constitution of the psyche, sexuality and the production of subjectivity.

Equivalences and binary systems

In the course of this text, we have seen that the analysis of theories on women and the feminine reveals essentialist notions, binary dilemmas and equivalences whose scope and effects we need to elucidate. Although these categories are intimately associated with concepts already developed in other chapters, we will now discuss them all together.

The logic of masculine-feminine polarity joins a series of equivalencies based on the Aristotelian model. In this model, the body referred only to the male's body, while the female's was presented as "the formless". Historically, Nature, the enigma, the emotions, the affects, the foreign, the object, lack, the wordless, the pre-linguistic, the pre-symbolic and the passive have been placed in the field of the feminine. On the contrary, in the field of the masculine we find culture, Reason, the centre, the norm, the subject, the symbolic and the active. Logocentrism organizes thinking around binary logic, in terms of oppositions and disjunctions. Although the thought processes are structured through this logic which we must inevitably use, we stress that on the way a slip occurs in which the categories mentioned before are equated and remain ascribed and fixed either to the masculine or the feminine. Consequently, this basic misunderstanding immobilizes certain characteristics in each of these fields. This limitation means that an effort is required to disassemble these equations and isomorphisms if we intend to clarify their effects on the construction of theories and on clinical practice.

A series of chains links these equivalence systems with the notion of the feminine as an enigmatic condition and with the concept of otherness. I think that the logic of considering women and the feminine an enigma is the root of most of the equations and slipped concepts concerning women. We point out that the field of hysteria lends itself to the construction and support of the enigma. Masculine castration phantasms are a complement to the hysterical enigma. In this line of thinking, the feminine enigma can only be considered an entity if hysteria is equated to femininity. At the same time, this equation is supported by an essentialist conception of the feminine, inherent in the plane of the Platonic essences.

As I said elsewhere (Glocer Fiorini, 2000), different and varied narratives provide stability and substance to the concept of feminine enigma. The notion of enigma in relation to the feminine is still supported by a mythical condition which largely explains its persistence. Myths provide codes articulating different planes of psychic and material reality. Their status is two-faced: one facet can obstruct significations while the other can inspire transformations. In addition, since myths remain fresh in the plot of social discourse, the myths of the past and the present coexist in the social imaginary. They also come together in the field of theory construction. Thus the feminine enigma comes into view as a mythical version of theoretical enunciates based on a heavy proposal: the lack of symbolization of the feminine. This notion is associated with the "thought of the negative" by way of categories of insufficiency, lack and emptiness. It is precisely this enigmatic condition that also functions as a barrier to the female's access to subjectivity.

How, then, can we find other conceptualizations which avoid assimilating the feminine condition to the pre-symbolic or the pre-linguistic, or to whatever is beyond language as an element indicative of difference? These conceptions tend to exalt the value of the enigma, thus closing the circle. This exaltation involves the risk of universalizing what is diverse and singular and, with a circular movement, tending to return to the pre-symbolic as a new form of feminine enigma. Therefore, returning to the questions in the first chapter, the first point is whether we need to consider the enigma as located in the field of the feminine; if so, the frame of phallic logic would thus be homogenizing these two categories: enigma and the feminine. In this case, we may conclude that the equation enigma = feminine becomes the object of displaced anxieties relating to the origins, the diverse, the sexual difference and the non-complementary character of desire.

The impasses generated by the concept of enigma, as well as these equations, are supported by dichotomous schemes of thought. These schemes, based on binary dilemmas, are of limited use because of their tendency to shut off problems by presenting false alternatives. If these alternatives respond to a strict assignment to the masculine or feminine side, they further obstruct these problems. *In view of this situation, we need to de-construct the equations of enigma. This means de-centring enigma from the field of the feminine, to which it still remains firmly attached.*

These systems of equivalences and displacements relate, as we have already stressed, to another misunderstanding: the feminine condition equated to the *Other*. This notion implies that the feminine is defined as such in relation to a centre, by a subject positioned as the subject of knowledge or the norm. We point out that the norm is an allusion to the Same: a totality without fissures. Notions, stereotypes and idealizations concerning the genders are shaped in this context, and the modes of thinking developed are based on oppositions, dichotomies and complementarities. *It is important to underscore that, whether as a complement or as a supplement, the feminine tends to be defined in relation to a given norm.*

We also need to emphasize that modifications in kinship systems and modes of filiation, in consonance with the development of new reproductive techniques, involve changes in subjectivity. As Tort (1992) points out: "these transformations affect the very structures of the symbolic systems governing the identification of subjects in all known societies (naming, filiation, maternity and paternity, sexual identity)." Therefore, we find that a field with imprecise limits is generated between new and possible forms of symbolic organization on the one hand and proposals tending to erase subjectivity on the other hand.

This context allows us to focus on the possibility of de-centring the categories of the Same from the Other. However, a thin line of conceptual slipping leads from the condition of otherness to the condition of object of exchange and "disposable object". The Father of the primitive horde, violent and all-powerful, possesses all the women, in the frame of a myth whose significations are revealing (Freud, 1913). This frame includes the conceptualization of women as objects of exchange according to the formulations of structural anthropology. In the theoretical scheme they configure, both women and words are exchangeable as a guarantee of symbolic order.

Consequently, in the polysemy inherent in the concept of the Other, we find a heavy element, inherent in the binary systems of the *episteme* of Modernity, which equates women and the feminine to the position of otherness. *Therefore, we need to de-sexualize otherness.* Unlinking the equation woman = Other assumes on the one hand recognition of the Other in the subject itself, and on the other hand the potential to recognize the Other as a subject.

We note that the concept of object-choice in relation to the oedipal resolution does not overlap the relation with the Other. The Other is neither a mere reference to the deceitful, mirrored other nor an absolute equivalent to the linguistic Other, although they are related. Further, otherness faces a radical heterogeneity that upsets the absolute certainties of the ego. This permits the subject to traverse experiences beyond narcissism and to surpass also the field of object relations.

In the itinerary we are reviewing, we find a mechanism of homogenization and equation of concepts: on the one hand, the enigma of difference is assigned to the feminine itself, while on the other hand, the feminine is displaced onto the condition of otherness. We have also highlighted these displacements as being deeply rooted in binary options. Binary systems and dichotomies are part of language, so we can neither annul nor evade them; it is therefore a question of exploring alternative ways and means to include them in larger complexities. The point of inflection is the production of "lines of flight" to break up rigid dualistic schemes (Deleuze, 1977). This involves "de-territorializing" and at the same time creating alternative territories which can be included in a field of multiplicities, whose only unity is based on their co-functioning. It also means salvaging a dimension of heterogeneity, countering strict dichotomies and oppositions as well as indiscriminate fusions of concepts. If we are to dismantle these relations, we also need to understand their determinations.

The binary conceptions lend themselves, precisely because of their dichotomous logic, to the exercise of relations of power-knowledge (Foucault, 1979). Inversely, power relations generate and organize binary relations. This adds further complexity since it introduces power relations as intrinsic elements of any relationship. Anxiety facing otherness and sexual difference promotes relations of domination and frequently immobilization in the masculine-feminine polarity. This may then be reproduced mechanically. At the roots of this immobilization we find the equation feminine = otherness.

Schemes of power adopt different shapes and configurations whose rationales vary according to contextual ideals. An invisible relational scheme is constituted between men and women, often materializing in acts of violence, but transcending this visible action. Violence appears in the frame of these relations of force, and its targets may be bodies, objects or beings which it changes, moulds or destroys. Violence is always an excess which both expresses and challenges the legislation on gender relations. In this context, we need to conceive areas of articulation with the phantasms of domination and subjection pertaining to each subject. These include forms organized around the dialectics of master and slave, the structuring in clinical configurations of sado-masochism, rapes, and other acts of explicit or implicit violence.

Between anatomical heterogeneity, gender diversity and sexual difference

We understand that the equivalences, isomorphisms and displacements we have described respond to logics with a powerful effect on subjectivity. This implies considering the conditions and ways in which they are organized and acquire psychic entity, and how they are processed metapsychologically. We need to recall that these categories have relations of concordance or discordance with the field of sexuality. We also emphasize that dismantling these equivalences does not mean ignoring symbolic sexual difference, but instead recognizing that this difference is beyond nature and is also supported by cultural determinations. As we will see, we should also distinguish between sexual difference and the category of difference itself, which is more encompassing and goes further in a symbolic sense. In our attempt to understand these relations, we will examine an imaginary space, the inter-subjective mother-child space, since upbringing—at least up to the present—is basically configured in these terms. In Winnicott's perspective, it can be considered a space of generation-*poiesis*, a third psychic space.

The newborn becomes a part of this initial intersection. Here, discourses circulate, in the manner of Bakhtin's concept (1963) of *dialogical principle*, as a polyphony of discourse, of several languages functioning at the same time. This polyphonic structure includes the word of the Other. In addition, discourse is discontinuous. Between what is said and what is concealed, between accepted and forbidden enunciations, effects of knowledge regarding sexual difference are signalled, with silences playing a fundamental part. This knowledge implies acceptance and resistance, qualifications and disqualifications, which act on the body and sexuality of the little girl. Aulagnier (1967) pointed out the splitting, frequent in women, between accepted knowledge about female sexuality and the truth of their unrecognized, often virtual desire.

The newborn is given a first name providing it with a distinct place in the linguistic field, in grammar, in syntax, and also a specific place in the social field and in culture. The infant is included in dispositions of alliance and kinship, in the frame of the symbolic systems accepted by each culture. The name outlines, distinguishes, pre-figures, marks, determines and indicates an origin. From the very beginning, the infant is positioned in an *initial diversity*: the field of the masculine or the feminine. Boys and girls are placed as such in an imaginary dimension where systems of ideals are configured concerning masculinity and femininity. This first great mental operation organizes identities and differences in a prefigured manner. Phantasmatic trajectories develop and myths and sagas are formed in connection with origins.

Diversity, in terms of masculine or feminine ideals, is intertwined with the ego/other relationship. The first other is the mother, and she is also the first object on the plane of desire. This relationship is the seed of mirroring and its ambition is sameness, while it is also the root of the diverse. In this first space of intersections, these categories meet but do not mix.

The field of pre-existing significations is different for boys and girls. The way a body ego is delimited is never neutral, but instead sexed, desiring and gendered. On this point, it is important to take note of the value of the paternal investment for the recognition of the daughter's femininity. The gaze is a source of libido which is distinctive for each sex and so it induces difference.

In the intersubjective space, ideals take shape regarding the modes and itineraries of desire, the permitted and forbidden pleasures, the body and its privacy or exhibition, and the place of affects and emotions; and these are different for girls and boys. This does not imply a direct relation with cultural discourses, but that ideals are constituted by multiple and subtle articulations with the maternal and paternal Other, their dreams and desires. The parents' modes of relating to the symbolic universe lead to greater or lesser submission to accepted stereotypes.

Green (1982) considers that mutative organizers and relays are superimposed on biological development. He points out that a bi-sexual phantasm, in relation to the primary scene, introduces a discordant factor with respect to the initial proposal: masculine or feminine. Thus, what is generated always differs from initial conditions and determinations. We find that multiple planes of organization develop:

1. the sex assigned to the newborn, in a pre-extant symbolic-imaginary universe,
2. the constitution of ideal identifications concerning gender on an imaginary plane,
3. the development of a bi-sexual phantasm,
4. the organization centring on the oedipal narrative and its resolution.

In the course of this development, diversity is accessed for the first time in terms of ideals concerning masculinity or femininity, which may or may not coincide with the sexed body. Also, when gender diversity encounters the field of drive and desire, different alternatives are determined. Their relation with mechanisms of repression and disavowal signals varying degrees of intrapsychic and inter-subjective conflict and discomfort.

For Laplanche (1980), pre-castration knowledge of gender distinction exists; it precedes access to sexual difference and has no drive value. He considers that this diversity responds to a kind of opposition of contrary elements, and that it can exist between two, but also among n elements. On the contrary, sexual difference is governed by the logic of contradiction inherent in duality and polarity, involving only two terms. In the same line of thinking, Bleichmar (1984) points out that both gender difference and sexual difference occur on the side of the preconscious; in the unconscious, representations coexist and only become contradictory when they attack the preconscious, that is to say the ego guided by the secondary process logic.

As I said before (2000), my intention is to apply these distinctions in a broader sense and re-formulate them; I propose to distinguish three concepts: *anatomical heterogeneity, identifying diversity* and *sexual difference*.

On the plane of *anatomical heterogeneity*, we have stressed that biological sex is not simply a natural fact; it is a construction to which medical, philosophical and religious narratives add significations and interpretation. This interpretation acquires theoretical validity and becomes part of a given *praxis* only in a discourse context that grants it pertinence. Also, an initial displacement from the biological body to the erogenous zones decentres the naturalist postulations.

As soon as the child is born, the sexed body begins to constitute a human fact which exceeds the field of nature. However, as a material reality it also constitutes a limit whose specificity cannot be reduced to the interpretive field. Material and psychic realities cross without becoming homogenized. The question is whether there is adaptation or bedrock between them. In addition, there are some aspects of the sexed body that are linked to the wordless, the archaic, as we saw in the first two chapters.

Concerning the notion of *diversity*, we find different interpretive lines. I use this concept in a very precise sense, different from sexual difference. I am not referring to ethnic, religious or class diversities. In the frame I propose, *diversity* is a reference to masculine or feminine imaginary ideals, partly unconscious and partly preconscious, which are eventually symbolized as ego ideal. Cultural conventions, ideal agencies and the parental unconscious provide signifiers which mark the infant's gender. This lends a feeling of imaginary unity, with a sexual attribution. Ideals and values of different signs concerning masculinity and femininity are embodied through the parents' identifying project, later becoming part of the ideal ego-ego ideal line. Between the access to sexual difference in the parents and the knowledge of gender diversity in the child—before his own access to difference—an intermediate space of knowledge-ignorance is generated. The child's imaginary conviction co-exists with the symbolic parental marks.

Thus an initial imaginary position is organized into a "before" the access to sexual difference, without confronting incompleteness. This "before" reminds us of the problem of temporality, which is central in psychoanalysis. Between the lineal quality of chronology and the non-temporal quality of the unconscious lies a broad field of theoretical developments and debates, which includes the concept of re-signification (deferred effect). For Green (1975), time is split into the time of the subject and the time of the Other; this generates a conflictive "heterochronia" with different potential between them. He points out that the time of the phantasm which lies between these two de-synchronizes natural order. It regulates exchanges between the child and the mother, and though it belongs to neither of them, together they generate a new time: transitional time.

These developments emphasize the importance of categorizing what is *between* terms, since this could be more important than the terms themselves. Therefore, the "before" antecedes the access to sexual difference in the subject and is re-signified by him/her; at the same time, it is a consequence of the parents' access to the symbolic difference. Moreover, the access to sexual difference implies each subject's previous positions concerning the diversity of genders. That is to say the configurations of these categories imply no lineal temporal succession, though they do include it.

In the frame of these discussions, we stress that the notion of gender diversity should not be equated to that of different and plural subjectivities. The concept of gender diversity is a reference to masculine-feminine polarities, and recognizes combinations which exceed binary systems, although these combinations are not arbitrary at all. On the other hand, the concept of multiple subjectivities concerns the various planes that intervene in the production of subjectivity, while accepting that these multiplicities also pass through dualist systems.

In addition, *sexual difference* is a notion pertaining to the field of desire and object choice. The access to difference is a symbolic operation involving the subject's insertion into a network of social ties with strong and effective imaginary components. This symbolic relational order precedes the subject, but the latter must be included in it as a condition to have access to subjectivity. As it is a symbolic operation, it is asexual, although it adopts historically varying versions and rationales concerning sexual difference.

Its mythical version, the Oedipus complex, is a metaphorical version of one of the ways in which the subject may be inserted into culture, with a legislation that psychoanalysis theorizes by means of the prohibition of incest and exogamic object choice. In psychoanalytic narrative, the interplay of identifications and object choices in the complete Oedipus complex presents diverse identification paths and sexual orientations.

From diversity to difference and from difference to another order of diversities, one or more symbolic operations are developed. There is an insistence on limiting the access to a symbolic universe to *one* constitutive operation. This operation pertains to the phallic phase and corresponds to an interplay of presence/absence—figured according to the infantile sexual theories in terms of phallus/castration. This prevents us from including it in logics of complexity and also from unravelling its significations. In the attempt to justify the phallus/castration explanation, an overlapping is produced between the philosophical notion of difference according to Heidegger, which is the opposite of totality and has a broader meaning, and the psychosexual difference. Psychoanalysis provides a metaphoric response, which has value within certain coordinates.

In addition, if the problem of human exchange demands a symbolic operation in terms of presence-absence, and if this implies that sexual difference is interpreted as a binary operation by the infantile sexual organization, in what terms do we explain adult organization? We require a *new movement* which considers diversity not only on an imaginary plane but in relation to a symbolic edge. In a broader sense, we need to conceptualize the category of difference as an asexuated operation, while bearing in mind that it is inevitably configured as being covered by significations. *These considerations do not imply the annulment of the sexual figures and their differences, but the inclusion and understanding of their determinations, contingencies and permanent elements. In this sense, the difference between subjects as well as the acceptance of the Other go even further than sexual difference.* This movement transcends the phallic monism of infantile sexual theories and also the anatomical sexual difference, both of which are re-articulated in a greater complexity. They are not homogeneous realities. Each of these planes incompletely explains one aspect of them.

In the course of these considerations, we find that the concept of *difference* in the psychoanalytic field is not univocal. It comes into play on different planes: from the Freudian description of infantile sexual theories, as an imaginary construction of sexual difference around the concept of the phallic phase, to the Oedipus-castration complex, as a proposal for understanding symbolic access to sexual difference through a binary operation; and from the concept of difference as conceived by Jones and other authors, based on a primary register of femininity, to the emphasis, in Lacanian theory, on difference in language as a signifying difference. These theories are not concordant, each offering us one order of answers while also generating new questions.

Some theoretical currents accentuate the notion of difference from other perspectives: they propose the importance of feminine writing or of a language "in the feminine"; other lines centre difference on corporeal eroticism. We think that if difference is centred only on the body or on pleasures, it encourages representational exclusion of the feminine.

It is interesting to recall that, for Deleuze (1980),[1] the category of difference refers to intensities of forces. Repetition is produced precisely when intensities are homogenized. These categories can be interpreted within this author's differentiation between the planes of organization and of consistency. In addition, if we use the notion of difference in a Heideggerian sense, as distinction or divergence, as the opposite of the One or of Totality, we can relate it to the psychoanalytic field. This would be the meaning of the subject's insertion in a symbolic universe: difference and distinction are generated to counter the "viscosity" and inertia of repetition.

Therefore, anatomical heterogeneity, gender diversity and sexual difference have relations of conjunction and disjunction, configuring non-sequential but coexisting logical organizations that do not necessarily reach a dialectic synthesis. These planes can be heterogeneous and conflictive, without diluting symbolic difference. They are neither abstract nor neutral concepts, being affected by discourse and knowledge about sexuality and gender current ideals. These factors in turn intersect with the effects of unconscious desire, which always breaks out in excess, in relation to an established order. Therefore, we need to discriminate these registers in order to illuminate the logics and conceptions at work, so that we can deconstruct categories considered universal, fixed or essential, and relativize the substantial or eternal character of ideals. We also need to remember that effective imaginary dimensions operate inside symbolic organization.

Between the bedrock of material reality, the heterogeneity of the unconscious phantasm and the field of social discourse, each of which limits the other, a field of intermediation, concordant or opposing, is simultaneously created. When we consider three or more variables and their combinations, we de-centre the hegemony of essential truths and lineal determinations. The intersections of these registers at the "between-two" and the "outside the two", enables the production of subjectivity to develop. At the intersections, we find phenomena of double capture, crossed lines and meeting points, like conversation rather than articulation (Deleuze, 1977). It means including binary systems in growing multiplicities, making language run between dualistic terms. It also means working on lines which support heterogeneous oppositions that would be incompatible with formal logic. It assumes the interplay of binary logic with logic of paradox and heterogeneity. These proposals lead us to think in terms of subjectivity "in process", as a "becoming" which is never the same but moves constantly towards the production of difference.

Note

1. For Deleuze, the plane of organization concerns both the development of the forms and the formation of subjects, and is structural and genetic; one plane of this type is that of the Law. Another type of plane is that of consistency. This plane knows only relations of movement and rest, speed and slowness among unformed elements, particles swept along by flows and affected by intensities. The plane of consistency points out events in terms of becoming or processes.

BIBLIOGRAPHY AND REFERENCES

Abelin Sas, G. (1994). The headless woman: Scheherazade's sorrows. In: A.K. Richards & A.D. Richards (Eds.), *The spectrum of Psychoanalysis*. Madison, Conn.: International Universities Press.

Alizade, A. (1992). *La sensualidad femenina*. Buenos Aires: Amorrortu.

André, J. (1994). *Sur la sexualité féminine*. Paris: Presses Universitaires de France.

André, J. (1995). *Aux origines féminines de la sexualité*. Paris: PUF.

Assoun, P.-L. (1993). *Freud y la mujer*. Buenos Aires: Nueva Visión, 1994 [*Freud et la femme*. Paris: Calmann-Levy].

Assoun, P.-L. (2005). *Lecciones psicoanalíticas sobre masculino y femenino*. Buenos Aires: Nueva Visión, 2006 [*Leçons psychanalytiques sur masculin et féminin*. Paris: Anthropos].

Aulagnier-Spairani, P. (1967). Observaciones sobre la femineidad y sus avatars. In: *El deseo y la perversión*. Buenos Aires: Sudamericana [*Le désir et la perversion*. Paris: Seuil].

Bakhtin M. (1963), *Problems of Dostoevsky's Poetics*. University of Minnesota Press, 1984.

Balandier, G. (1988). *El desorden*. Barcelona: Gedisa, 1990 [*Le désordre*. Paris: Fayard].

Baranger, W., Goldstein, N. & Zak de Goldstein, R. (1989). Acerca de la desidentificación. *Rev Psicoanál 46/6*: 895–903.

Bart, P.B., (1979). Depresión en mujeres de mediana edad. In: Carmen Sáez, *Mujer, locura y feminismo*. Madrid: Dédalo.

Baudrillard, J. (1990). *The Transparency of Evil*. London: Verso, 1993.

Braidotti, R. (2004). *Feminismo, diferencia sexual y subjetividad nómade*. Barcelona: Gedisa.

144   BIBLIOGRAPHY AND REFERENCES

Benjamin, J. (1988). *The bonds of love: Psychoanalysis, feminism and the problem of domination*. New York: Pantheon.

Benjamin, W. (1936). *The Work of Art in the Age of Mechanical Reproduction*. http://www.marxists.org/reference/subject/philosophy/works/ge/benjamin.htm

Bleichmar, S. (1984). *En los orígenes del sujeto psíquico*. Buenos Aires: Amorrortu.

Bourdieu, P. (1998). *Masculine Domination*. Cambridge: Polity, 2001.

Bowlby, J. (1969). *Attachment and Loss*. London: Hogarth.

Burin, M. (1987). Vicisitudes de la reorganización pulsional en la crisis de la mediana edad en las mujeres. In: *Estudios sobre la subjetividad femenina*. Buenos Aires: Grupo Editor Latinoamericano.

Butler, J. (1990). *Gender Trouble*. New York: Routledge.

Castoriadis, C. (1986). *El psicoanálisis, proyecto y elucidación*. Buenos Aires: Nueva Visión, 1992.

Castoriadis, C. (1990). *World in Fragments*. Stanford, CA: Stanford University Press, 1997.

Castoriadis, C. (1998). *Figures of the Thinkable*. Stanford, CA: Stanford University Press, 2007.

Castoriadis-Aulagnier, P. (1975). *The Violence of Interpretation: From Pictogram to Statement*. Hove: Brunner/Routledge, 2001.

Chasseguet-Smirgel, J. (1964). Feminine guilt and the Oedipus complex. In: *Female sexuality: New Psychoanalytic Views*. London: Karnac, 1991.

Chodorow, N. (1978). *The reproduction of mothering*. Berkeley, CA: University of California Press.

Copjec, J. (2006). *El sexo y la eutanasia de la razón*. Paidós, Buenos Aires.

Cosnier, J. (1987). *Los destinos de la femineidad*. Madrid: Julián Yebenes, 1992 [*Destins de la féminité*. Paris: PUF].

David-Ménard, M. (1987). Identificación e hysteria. In: *Las identificaciones*. Buenos Aires: Nueva Visión, 1988 [*Les Identifications*. Paris: Denoel].

David-Ménard, M. (1997). *Las construcciones de lo universal*. Buenos Aires: Nueva Visión, 1999 [*Les Constructions de l'universel*. Paris: PUF].

De Beauvoir, S. (1949). *The Second Sex*. Penguin, 1972.

Deleuze, G. (1972), *Proust and signs*. Penguin, 1973.

Deleuze, G. (1986), *Foucault*. London: Athlone, 1988.

Deleuze, G. (1995), *Conversaciones*. Valencia: Pre-Textos.

Deleuze, G. & Parnet, C. (1977), *Dialogues*. London: Athlone, 2002.

Deleuze, G.-Guattari, F. (1980), *Mil Mesetas*. Valencia: Pre-Textos, 1994.

Dío Bleichmar, E. (1985). *El feminismo espontáneo de la histeria*. Madrid: Adotraf.

Dolto, F. (1982). *Sexualidad femenina.* Buenos Aires: Paidós, 1983 [*La sexualité féminine.* Paris: Scarabée].

Duby, G. & Perrot, M. (1990). *History of Women in the West.* Vol. 1. Harvard University Press, 1992.

Duvignaud, F. (1981), *El cuerpo del horror.* Fondo de Cultura Económica, México, 1987 [*Le corps de l'effroi.* Paris: Le Sycomore].

Eco, U. (1962), *The Open Work.* London: Hutchinson, 1989.

Eliade, M. (1955), *Images and symbols.* Princeton University Press, 1991.

Elliott, A. (1992). *Social Theory and Psychoanalysis in Transition.* Oxford: Blackwell.

Elliott, A. (1996): *Subject to Ourselves: Social Theory, Psychoanalysis and Postmodernity.* London: Polity.

Erasmus of Rotterdam (1511). *The Praise of Folly.* Penguin Classics, 1993.

Faure-Oppenheimer, A. (1980), *La elección de sexo.* Madrid: Akal, 1986 [*Le choix du sexe.* Paris: PUF].

Fernandez, A.M. (1992). La diferencia en psicoanálisis: ¿Teoría o ilusión? In: *Las mujeres en la imaginación colectiva.* Buenos Aires: Paidós.

Fiorini, H. (1999). La clínica a la luz de las nuevas epistemologías: modelos de la complejidad. In: *Nuevas líneas en psicoterapias psicoanalíticas.* Madrid: Psimática.

Flax, J. (1990). *Thinking Fragments: Psychoanalysis, Feminism and Postmodernism in the Contemporary West.* Berkeley: University of California Press.

Fonagy, P., Krause, R. & Leuzinger-Bohleber, M. (2006). *Identity, Gender and Sexuality: 150 Years After Freud.* London: International Psychoanalytical Association.

Foucault, M. (1966), *The Order of Things.* London: Routledge, 2001.

Foucault, M. (1979), *Microfísica del poder.* Madrid: La Piqueta, 1991.

Foucault, M. (1984), *The History of Sexuality 1: The Will to Knowledge.* Penguin, 1998.

Fox Keller, E. (1993). The paradox of scientific subjectivity. In: D. Fried Schnitman & J. Schnitman (Eds.), *New Paradigms, Culture and Subjectivity.* Cresskill, NJ: Hampton Press, 2001.

Freud, S. (1900). The Interpretation of Dreams. *S.E., 4–5.*

Freud, S. (1905 [1901]). Fragment of an Analysis of a Case of Hysteria. *S.E., 7:* 3–122.

Freud, S. (1905). Three Essays on the Theory of Sexuality. *S.E., 7:* 125–245.

Freud, S. (1910). A Special Type of Choice of Object made by Men. *S.E., 11:* 165–175.

Freud, S. (1911). Psycho-Analytic Notes on an Autobiographical Account of a Case of Paranoia (Dementia Paranoides). *S.E., 12:* 3–82.

Freud, S. (1912). On the Universal Tendency to Debasement in the Sphere of Love. *S.E.*, *11*: 179–190.

Freud, S. (1913 a). The Theme of the Three Caskets. *S.E.*, *12*: 289–301.

Freud, S. (1913 b). Totem and Taboo. *S.E.*, *13*: 1–161.

Freud, S. (1914). On Narcissism: An Introduction. *S.E.*, *14*: 73–102.

Freud, S. (1915). Instincts and their Vicissitudes. *S.E.*, *14*: 111–140.

Freud, S. (1916–17). General Theory of the Neuroses. Introductory Lectures on Psychoanalysis. *S.E.*, *16*: 243–477.

Freud, S. (1917). On Transformations of Instinct as Exemplified in Anal Erotism. *S.E.*, *17*: 125–133.

Freud, S. (1918 [1917]). The Taboo of Virginity. Contributions to the Psychology of Love, III. *S.E.*, *11*: 193–208.

Freud, S. (1919). The Uncanny. *S.E.*, *17*: 219–256.

Freud, S. (1920). The Psychogenesis of a Case of Homosexuality in a Woman. *S.E.*, *18*: 147–172.

Freud, S. (1921). Group Psychology and the Analysis of the Ego. *S.E.*, *18*: 67–143.

Freud, S. (1923a). The Infantile Genital Organization: An Interpolation into the Theory of Sexuality. *S.E.*, *19*: 141–145.

Freud, S. (1923b). The Ego and the Id. *S.E.*, *19*: 3–66.

Freud, S. (1924). The Dissolution of the Oedipus Complex. *S.E.*, *19*: 171–179.

Freud, S. (1925). Some Psychical Consequences of the Anatomical Distinction between the Sexes. *S.E.*, *19*: 243–258.

Freud, S. (1926). *The Question of Lay Analysis. S.E.*, *20*: 179–258.

Freud, S. (1930 [1929]). Civilization and its Discontents. *S.E.*, *21*: 59–145.

Freud, S. (1931). Female Sexuality. *S.E.*, *21*: 223–243.

Freud, S. (1933 [1932]). Femininity. New Introductory Lectures on Psychoanalysis. *S.E.*, *22*: 112–135.

Freud, S. (1937a). Constructions in Analysis. *S.E.*, *23*:257–269.

Freud, S. (1937b). Analysis Terminable and Interminable. *S.E.*, *23*: 211–253.

Freud, S. (1940 [1922]). Medusa´s Head. *S.E.*, *18*: 273–274.

Freud, S. (1940 [1938]). An Outline of Psychoanalysis. *S.E.*, *23*: 139–207.

Glocer Fiorini, L. (1994). La posición femenina. Una construcción heterogénea. *Rev. de Psicoanálisis, 51/3*: 587–603.

Glocer Fiorini, L. (1998). The feminine in Psychoanalysis: A complex construction. *Journal of Clinical Psychoanalysis, 7*: 421–439.

Glocer Fiorini, L. (2000). El enigma de la diferencia. In: A. M. Alizade (Ed.), *Escenarios femeninos*. Buenos Aires: Lumen.

Glocer Fiorini, L. (2001). *Lo femenino y el pensamiento complejo*. Buenos Aires: Lugar Editorial.

Glocer Fiorini, L. (2001). El deseo de hijo: de la carencia a la producción deseante. *Rev. de Psicoanálisis, 53/4*, 965–976.

Glocer Fiorini, L. (2002). Fertilización asistida. Nuevas problemáticas. In: E. Wolfberg (Ed.), *Prevención en Salud Mental*. Buenos Aires: Lugar Editorial.

Glocer Fiorini, L. (2004). *El Otro en la Trama Intersubjetiva*. Buenos Aires: Lugar Editorial.

Glocer Fiorini, L. (2004). Sexualidad y género. Convergencias y divergencias. In: *Psicoanálisis y relaciones de género*. Buenos Aires: Lumen.

Glocer Fiorini, L. (2005). Trauma, violencia sexual y relaciones de poder. *Revista de Psicoanálisis, 62/2*: 291–304.

Glocer Fiorini, L. (2006). The bodies of present-day maternity. In: *Motherhood in the Twenty-First Century*. London: Karnac.

Glocer Fiorini, L. & Gimenez de Vainer, A. (2003). The sexed body and the real: its meaning in transsexualism. In: A.M. Alizade (Ed.), *Masculine Scenarios*. London: Karnac.

Goldstein, R. Zak de (1984). The dark continent and its enigmas. *International Journal of Psycho-Analysis 65*: 179–189.

Granoff, W. & Perrier, F. (1964). *El problema de la perversión en la mujer*. Barcelona: Crítica, 1980 [Le problème de la perversion chez la femme et les idéaux féminins. *Psychanalyse 7*: 141–199].

Green, A. (1975). Le temps mort. *Nouvelle Revue de Psychanalyse 11*: 103–110.

Green, A. (2002). *The Chains of Eros*. London: Karnac.

Green, A. (1982). El género neutron. In: J.-B. Pontalis et al, *Bisexualidad y diferencia de los sexos*. Buenos Aires: Ed. del 80 [J.-B. Pontalis et al, *Bisexualité et différence des sexes*. Paris: Gallimard, 2000].

Greenson, R. (1968). Dis-identifying from mother, its special importance for the boy. *Int. J. Psychoanal., 49/ 2–3*: 370–374.

Grunberger, B. (1964). Outline for a study of narcissism in female sexuality. In: J. Chasseguet-Smirgel, *Female sexuality: New Psychoanalytic Views*. London: Karnac, 1991.

Guattari, F. (1992). *Chaosmosis*. Indiana University Press, 1995.

Guillaumin, J. (1979). Observaciones para una metodología general de las investigaciones sobre las crisis. In: R. Kaës et al (Eds.), *Crisis, ruptura y superación*. Buenos Aires: Cinco [Pour une méthodologie générale des recherches sur les crises. In: R. Kaës et al (Eds.), *Crise, rupture et dépassement*. Paris: Dunod].

Harris, M. (1974). *Cows, Pigs Wars and Witches: The Riddles of Culture*. New York: Vintage, 1989.

Héritier, F. (1996). *Masculino/Femenino. El pensamiento de la diferencia*. Editorial Ariel, Barcelona, 2002 [*Masculin/féminin: La pensée de la différence*. Paris: Odile Jacob].

Horney, K. (1924). *Feminine Psychology.* New York: Norton, 1993.

Irigaray, L. (1977). *This Sex Which Is Not One.* New York: Cornell University Press, 1985.

Irigaray, L. (1992). On the maternal order. In: *Je, tu, nous: Toward a culture of difference.* New York: Routledge, 1993.

Israël, L. (1979). *La histeria, el sexo y el médico.* Barcelona: Toray-Masson.

Jacques, E. (1974). Mort et crise du milieu de la vie. In: D. Anzieu et al, *Psychanalysedu genie créateur.* Paris: Dunod.

Jones, E. (1927). The early development of female sexuality. *Int. J. Psychoanal.* 8: 459–472.

Juranville, A. (1984). *Lacan et la philosophie.* Paris: PUF.

Kaës, R. (1979). "Introducción al análisis transicional", en *Crisis, ruptura y superación.* Buenos Aires: Cinco. [Introduction à l'analyse transitionnelle. In: *Crise, rupture et dépassement.* Paris: Dunod].

Klein, M. (1945). The Oedipus Complex in the Light of Early Anxieties. *International Journal of Psycho-Analysis,* 26: 11–33.

Kristeva, J. (1980). *Powers of Horror.* New York: Columbia University Press, 1982.

Kristeva, J. (1983a). Stabat Mater. In: *Tales of Love.* New York: Columbia University Press, 1987.

Kristeva, J. (1983b). Narcissus: the new insanity. In: *Tales of Love.* New York: Columbia University Press, 1987.

Kristeva, J. (1986). Revolution in poetic language. In: Toril Moi (Ed.), *The Kristeva Reader.* Oxford: Blackwell.

Kristeva, J. (1988). *Strangers to Ourselves.* London: Harvester Wheatsheaf, 1991.

Kristeva, J. (1992). El ritual galante. Interview in *Rev. de Occidente.* 133: 98–114.

Kofman S. (1980). *The Enigma of Woman: Woman in Freud's Writings.* Ithaca, NY: Cornell University Press.

Lacan, J. (1956). The hysteric's question (II): What is a woman? In: *The Seminar, Book III: The Psychoses.* London: Norton, 1993.

Lacan, J. (1958a). The signification of the phallus. In: *Écrits.* London: Norton, 2007.

Lacan, J. (1958b), *The Seminar, Book V: The Formations of the Unconscious.* London: Karnac, 2002.

Lacan, J. (1960). *The Seminar, Book VII: The Ethics of Psychoanalysis 1959–1960.* London: Routledge, 1992.

Lacan, J. (1960). Guiding Remarks for a Convention on Female Sexuality. In: *Écrits.* London: Norton, 2007.

Lacan, J. (1966). The Function and Field of Speech and Language in Psychoanalysis. In: *Écrits.* London: Norton, 2007.

Lacan, J. (1972–73). *The Seminar, Book XX: Encore*. London: Norton, 2000.

Laks Eizirik, C. (2002). Contexto histórico y cultural de lo masculino y de lo femenino: Una visión psicoanalítica. *Trópicos, 10/2*: 28–34.

Langer, M. (1951). *Maternidad y Sexo*. Buenos Aires: Paidós, 1964.

Laplanche, J. & Pontalis, J. B. (1967). *The Language of Psychoanalysis*. London: Karnac, 1988.

Laplanche J. (1969–70). *La Sexualidad*. Buenos Aires: Nueva Visión, 1980.

Laplanche J. (1980). *Problématiques II : Castration-Symbolisations*. Paris, PUF.

Laqueur, T. (1990). Making sex: Body and gender from the Greeks to Freud. Cambridge, Mass.: Harvard University Press.

Leclaire, S. (1998). *Écrits pour la psychanalyse, I*. Paris: Seuil.

Lévesque, C. (2002). *Par-delà le masculin et le féminin*. Paris: Aubier.

Lévine, É. & Touboul, P. (2002). *Le corps*. Paris: Flammarion.

Levinas, E. (1947). *Time and the Other*. Pittsburgh: Duquesne University Press, 1990.

Lévi-Strauss, C. (1949). *The Elementary Structures of Kinship*. Beacone Press, 1977.

Liberman, A. (2000). Elektra o la amoralidad del amor. In: *Música, el exilio acompañado*. Valladolid Simancas.

Lorite Mena, J. (1987). *El orden femenino. Origen de un simulacro cultural*. Barcelona: Anthropos.

Lyon, D. (1994). *Postmodernity*. Buckingham: Open University Press.

Mack Brunswick, R. (1940). The preoedipal phase of the libido development. *Psychoanalytic Quarterly, 9*: 293–319.

Marini, M. (1986). *Jacques Lacan: The French context*. Rutgers University Press, 1993.

Mayer, H. (1989). *Volver a Freud*. Buenos Aires: Paidós.

Marzano, M. (2003). *La pornographie ou l'épuisement du désir*. Paris: Buchet-Chastel.

Mc Dougall, J. (1989). The Dead Father. *Int J. Psycho-Anal. 70/2*:205–19.

Méantis, G. (1964). *Mitología griega*. Buenos Aires: Hachette.

Mitchell, J. & Rose, J. (1982). *Feminine sexuality: Jacques Lacan and the école freudienne*. New York: Norton.

Melman, C. (1985). *Nuevos estudios sobre la histeria*. Buenos Aires: Letra Viva.

Moi, T. (1986). *The Kristeva Reader*. Oxford: Blackwell.

Money, J., Hampson, J.G. & Hampson, J.L. (1957). Imprinting and the establishment of gender role. *Arch. Neurol. Psychiat., 77*: 333–336.

Montrelay, M. (1974). Investigaciones sobre la femineidad. In: Juan D. Nasio (Comp.), *Acto Psicoanalítico*. Buenos Aires: Nueva Visión.

Morin, E. (1977). *El método I. La naturaleza de la naturaleza*. Madrid: Cátedra, 1986 [*La Méthode: La nature de la nature*].

Morin, E. (1986), *El método III. El conocimiento del conocimiento*. Madrid: Cátedra, 1988 [*La Méthode: La connaissance de la connaissance*].

Morin, E. (1990), *Introducción al pensamiento complejo*. Barcelona: Gedisa, 1995 [*Introduction à la pensée complexe*].

Muller, J. (1932). A Contribution to the Problem of Libidinal Development of the Genital Phase in Girls. *International Journal of Psychoanalysis, XIII*: 361–368.

Nasio J.D. (1996). *Los gritos del cuerpo*. Buenos Aires: Paidós, 1997.

Nicholson, L.J. (1990). *Feminism/Postmodernism*. New York: Routledge.

Ovid. *The Metamorphoses*. Penguin Classics, 2004.

Plato. *The Symposium*. Penguin Classics, 2003.

Pommier, G. (1985). *La excepción femenina*. Buenos Aires: Alianza, 1986.

Pontalis, J-B. (1973). El inasible a medias. In: *Bisexualidad y diferencia de los sexos*. Buenos Aires: Ed. del 80, 1982 [*Bisexualité et différence des sexes*. Paris: Gallimard].

Riviere J. (1929). Womanliness as Masquerade. *International Journal of Psychoanalysis, 10*: 303–317.

Roudinesco, E. (2002). *La familia en desorden*. Fondo de Cultura Económica, Buenos Aires, 2003 [*La famille en désordre*. Paris: Fayard].

Rousseau, J-J. (1762). *The Social Contract*. Penguin Classics, 1969.

Rubin, G. (1975). The traffic in women: notes on the "political economy" of sex. In: Rayne R. Reiter (Ed.), *Toward an Anthropology of Women*. New York: Monthly Review Press.

Sáez, C. (1979). *Mujer, locura y feminismo*. Madrid: Dédalo.

Schopenhauer A. (1966). *El amor, las mujeres y la muerte*. Madrid: EDAF.

Sobchak V. (1994). The revenge of the leech woman. In: *Uncontrollable bodies*. Seattle: Bay Press.

Spector Person, E. (2002). Sexo, género y el inconsciente cultural. *Trópicos, 10/2*: 84–95.

Stoller, R. (1968). *Sex and Gender*. London: Karnac,1984.

Todorov, T. (1995). *La vida en común*. Madrid: Taurus.

Torok, M. (1964). The significance of penis envy in women. In J. Chasseguet-Smirgel, *Female sexuality: New Psychoanalytic Views*. London: Karnac, 1991.

Tort, M. (1991). Lo que un sexo sabe del otro. In: *El ejercicio del saber y la diferencia de los sexos*. Buenos Aires: Ed de la Flor, 1993 [G. Fraisse et al, *L'Exercice du Savoir et la Différence des Sexes*. Paris: L'Harmattan].

Tort, M. (1992). *El deseo frío*. Buenos Aires: Nueva Visión, 1994. [*Le désir froid: Procréation artificielle et crise des repères symboliques*. Paris: La Découverte].

Trías, E. (1982). *Lo bello y lo siniestro*. Barcelona: Seix Barral, 1984.

Trías, E. (1983). *Filosofía del futuro*. Barcelona: Destino, 1995.

Trías, E. (1991). *Lógica del límite*. Barcelona: Destino.

Tubert S. (1991). *Mujeres sin sombra*. Madrid: Siglo veintiuno.

Tyson, P. (1997). Sexuality, Femininity, and Contemporary Psychoanalysis. *Int. J. Psycho-Anal., 78*: 385–389

Vattimo, G. (1980) *The Adventure of Difference: Philosophy after Nietzsche and Heidegger*. Baltimore: John Hopkins University Press, 1993.

Vattimo, G. (1990), Posmodernidad: ¿Una sociedad transparente? In *En torno a la posmodernidad*. Anthropos. Barcelona. 1991.

Winnicott, D. (1959). The Fate of the Transitional Object. In: *Psycho-Analytic Explorations*. London: Karnac, 1989.

Winnicott, D. (1966). The Split-off Male and Female Elements to be Found in Men and Women. In: *Psycho-Analytic Explorations*. London: Karnac, 1989.

Woolf, V. (1928). *Orlando*. Oxford Paperbacks, 1998.

Wright, E. (1992). *Feminism and Psychoanalysis: A Critical Dictionary*. Oxford: Blackwell.

Zizek, S (1994). *The metastases of enjoyment*. London: Verso.

Zolla, E. (1981). *Androginia*. Madrid: Debate, 1990.

INDEX